JOHN REED
OBE

A PICTORIAL BIOGRAPHY
by Ian G Smith

In his words, mine and those of many others

John Reed

Acknowledgments

To John's partner, Nicholas Kerri for supporting the venture and providing me with many of the pictures featured in this Pictorial Biography. To others who kindly supplied photographs.

To Martin from my own design studio and Lez from RDS Design for the interest and enthusiasm in ensuring it is a book worth looking at!

Copyright c 2010 by Ian G Smith

ISBN Hardcover: 978-0-9553707-1-7

Printed by PLATINUM   **www.platinumprint.com**

Nicki enjoyed appearing with John in a number
of cameo roles. Here they are in the New York "Iolanthe."

Dedicated

This book celebrates

*True Gilbert and Sullivan lovers everywhere – who, like me,
recognise the unique talent of John Reed OBE.*

*The thousands of people who support our International Gilbert
and Sullivan Festivals in Buxton, UK, and now in Gettysburg, USA.
Your continued support helps us achieve our goal of keeping
the Gilbert and Sullivan candles burning brightly on both sides
of the Atlantic.*

*Janet for encouraging me to complete something which I began in
2001, in time for the 2010 International Festival.*

*I am sure you will find "typos", "errors" and "omissions."
For those I apologise in advance.*

*I can assure you I have made every effort
to ensure the authenticity of content and illustrations.*

John Reed

Contents

"MUST HAVE A BEGINNING YOU KNOW"

Foreword

I was in Gettysburg, USA the night that John Reed died - planning a Festival of Gilbert and Sullivan in the United States. To say that I was upset was an understatement. I had known John as a friend for as long as he had been with the D'Oyly Carte Opera Company – 28 years. Like all friends we had our high moments and low moments. We shared successes – and disappointments. But whenever we met, disappointments were forgotten and very quickly John, who in latter years did not enjoy the best of health, would be sitting up alive and alert and full of past memories and future aspirations.

Back in 2002 and 2003 John and Nicki agreed that I could prepare John's autobiography. It would be a real labour of love. They handed me reams and reams of notes which they had prepared over the years and I sat down and began to piece together John's story. I wanted to publish and launch it at the Gilbert and Sullivan festival in 2003 but in early Spring was frankly running behind schedule. I was travelling for ten days in Holland and Belgium and decided that those ten evenings would give me the time to catch up. A full print out of what I had done was in my brief case along with my lap-top and notes that needed re-writing. The first three days of my travels took me to Wageningen University in the Netherlands, and I was pleased with the progress I made those evenings. I had to go on to meetings with the EU in Brussels and took the train – more time for editing and progressing the book.

I arrived in Brussels Midi Station just before 10p.m. I don't know why but I sensed quite an uncomfortable atmosphere as I took the escalator from platform to lobby to find a taxi. I sensed "shapes" on the platform and someone close behind me and clutched my suitcase and briefcase tightly. As I left the escalator someone spoke in broken English. "Excuse me sir have you seen the back of your raincoat. It looks like someone has poured liquid down it." Instinctively I stopped, and for a brief moment put my briefcase down and with my right hand pulled the raincoat up over my left shoulder. The man was right. A dreadful gooey substance was plain to see. The man offered me a pack of paper tissues – and it was only then I looked at him and saw an unkempt unshaven shabby - clothed individual offering me a pack of tissues. It did not seem right. I swung back to pick up my brief case.

Of course it had gone and I could see another man running down one of the many corridors. He was carrying my case – containing the only print out anyone had of the John Reed story; the paper files that I had taken with me and my laptop with the electronic version of the book.

What a horrible night. I gave chase but I was running with a suitcase and had no chance. I found the police and was taken to a nearby police station where I was told such things happened two or three times every night and that I should be grateful I had chased the man with my brief case rather than fight the one who offered me the tissues. Apparently he had head-butted the previous victim that evening and broken his nose. Small consolation. Scores of hours of work had gone and they were irreplaceable.

I was in the police station until the early hours and insisted that I should go back to the railway station at first light to check the waste bins. My laptop would certainly have gone and probably been sold by now but perhaps they had dumped the paperwork. I went back and was taken to the central refuse collection area. My heart sank again. It was half the size of a football pitch and full of rubbish –not just from the previous night but by the looks of it from many previous nights.

Got mine at
the G & S
Festival.
Hope you
enjoy it.

Jennifer.

Merry Christmas
& Happy New
Year.

fond love
Angela x

2011

I don't pretend to be a technical man and of course it had never entered my head to copy (or back up) what was on my computer. " Too late! Too late!" And the rest is history ......almost. Cynthia Morey, one of John's closest friends, agreed to start again from scratch and a first book "Nothing Whatever to Grumble At" was published in 2006.

Sitting in my bedroom in Gettysburg the night John died I began reading the early tributes that were being published following the announcement. They were all very moving. And for some strange reason I wanted to read what I had stored about John in recent years. I discovered that I had three "archive" files - "new archive," "old archive" and "the Old Vicarage archive." Apparently, when I got a new lap top a couple of years ago, our IT man had taken every file he could find of mine from our server and put them on my new machine. When I opened "The Old Vicarage" archive and looked at my folder of "John Reed" I could not believe my eyes. There was the story that had been stolen eight years ago. It had been hiding on our "hard drive" for all that time.

I decided there and then that if Nicki agreed, I would complete what I had begun. Sadly John would not see it but hopefully it would provide another perspective on his life – as a performer; as a director and as a friend. My book would include material from other people whose lives John touched and any proceeds from the book would go to our exciting youth programme which has now expanded from the UK to include the USA.

I know John would have approved of that.

9

John Reed - Savoyard by Colin Prestige

A theatrical engagement begins with an audition. So it was that on
2nd October, 1951, a certain John Reed was auditioned in Glasgow with
a view to joining the D'Oyly Carte Opera Company. He had previously
played many parts in musical comedy with the Darlington Operatic
Society - Darlington is his home town - and John had been in repertory
at Stockton, Redcar and Saltburn. In auditioning for the D'Oyly Carte
Company, on the recommendation of Eric Thornton, he was setting
his sights rather higher.

Those who conducted the audition were Eleanor Evans, Director of
Productions, Isidore Godfrey, Musical Director, and Jerome Stephens,
Stage Manager: surely 2nd October, 1951, was a fortunate day in the
annals of D'Oyly Carte when those three listened to a light baritone,
voice compass G to F, of good appearance and 'pleasant quality
of voice". Their verdict was endorsed a fortnight later, in Edinburgh
on 17th October, when Dame Bridget D'Oyly Carte and Mr. Frederic
Lloyd, at a second audition, thought him "very promising". He took
up his contract on 2nd November at Newcastle-upon-Tyne as a chorister
and understudy.

The Major

The Judge

Antonio

Mr Cox

Reed's first solo part was as the **Major** in "Patience" a role traditionally played by the comedy lead understudy. By March 1955 he was the **Judge** - "and a good Judge too" - in "Trial by Jury" and **Cox** in "Cox and Box". He was also playing other small roles at this time, such as **Antonio** in "The Gondoliers". Here he showed his great skill as a dancer, for the production of "The Gondoliers" at that time required an Antonio who could dance vigorously while singing "For the merriest fellows are we".

In the summer of 1959, Peter Pratt retired from his roles at the same time as illness compelled the late Ann Drummond-Grant to withdraw from the company. John Reed succeeded Pratt, supported by a new leading lady in Gillian Knight. It is never easy for an artist to wear the mantle of his predecessor (as Martyn Green found when he succeeded Sir Henry Lytton) but John Reed did not try to do so. He struck out on his own line, adapting his interpretations within the confines of the productions to his own magical stage personality. He invested his parts with wit, drive, inventiveness and subtlety.

When Reed took over his major roles, he dropped the Learned Judge. He resigned Major-General Stanley in 1968, but the 1970s brought him three new opportunities as John Wellington Wells in 1971, Scaphio in "Utopia Limited" in 1975 and Rudolph in "The Grand Duke" in the one-performance concert version that same centenary year (when he also resumed the Judge in the four Savoy performances of "Trial by Jury"). It was a privilege to play these three new roles, unhampered by memories of predecessors. His interpretations were entirely his own. To J. W. Wells (which I think he regarded as his toughest role) he brought a cockney insouciance, a mastery of dialogue and accuracy of enunciation, breath-taking fast patter and resigned pathos as he yielded to Ahrimanes.

As Scaphio he generously subordinated his playing to Kenneth Sandford's King Paramount. Yet he could still be witty, sly, sneaky and in his dancing, as always, neat and amusing. How neatly he timed his smiles, some of them sinister, some sardonic as Scaphio!

His career included many highlights of D'Oyly Carte history. One thinks of the hilarity and inventive wit at the **"Last Nights"** of London seasons. One never knew what unexpected delight would be produced. He has sung to Prime Ministers, Lord Chancellors and First Lords of the Admiralty. He has played before the Queen and other members of the Royal Family at least eight times, including of course the Silver Jubilee Command Performance at Windsor Castle of "H.M.S. Pinafore". When the Prince of Wales, aged 11, saw "The Mikado", Ko-Ko afterwards entertained him in the dressing-room.

Then, interspersed with touring in England, Wales, Scotland and Ireland, there were eleven overseas tours, exhausting occasions which demand much travelling and acceptance of social invitations when an artist would like to relax informally. Reed was a chorister in the 1955-56 tour to the United States and Canada, but it was as principal comedian that he ten times led the company overseas from 1962, culminating with the visit to Australia and New Zealand in 1979. The responsibility and physical exertions of these tours, with much air travel, are seldom appreciated, and to a sensitive artist the strain is considerable, yet it is John Reed's reward that he won many international admirers. It was altogether fitting that he was appointed an Officer of the Order of the British Empire in 1977.

Memory will want to recall just a few of his particular touches. One thinks of **Sir Joseph Porter**, proud, stiff and smug, who speaks with condescension and during the encores to the Act II trio signals in semaphore for help and jumps overboard (both these pieces of business he invented himself; he did not inherit them).

As the **Major-General**, he would sing his song effortlessly on the top of his voice at breath-taking speed. "A washing-bill in Babylonic cuneiform" is an absurdity: Reed makes the preposterous idea sound amusing.

Reginald Bunthorne, quietly persuasive, is sly in his singing of "If you're anxious" and selfish when he removes the engagement ring from Patience as Grosvenor arrives, in the Act I finale.

His **Lord Chancellor** had an inner humour and cheerful grin when bestowing pretty girls; it is a lawyer who speaks about affidavits and the rules of evidence; it is a friend who sings about excessive professional licence. There is a smile as he makes that exit. In the dance to the trio, he always delighted when he stops his unprofessional dance just before Lord Mountararat can reprove him. All in all, a study in which Reed can take "legitimate pride".

King Gama is an interpretation which I always enjoyed. How magnificently did Reed dominate stage and audience in that fine opening song   and the ensuing dialogue. Here Reed recalls a now past school of acting, when with crusty venom in his voice he baits Cyril and teases Hilarion. Dry, royal and waspish, note how he phrases the line "erring fellow creatures". Note too how Reed speaks with pride of the eight virtues of his daughter, leading up to the great climax of *"I am no snob"*.

Ko-Ko changed over the years. Once rather vapid, perhaps even light-weight, with elfin-like dancing, it matured into the cheap tailor out of his social depth.
He had the lightest of touches in "irritating laughs". There were nearly always topical and amusing substitutions for "the lady novelist" and "Knightsbridge" (for example, "Sadler's Wells", when that organisation started its own presentations, and "referendumist" at the time of the Common Market vote).
He dreamed up some new business for the encores to "Here's a how -de-do". Having delivered to Katisha his "white-hot passion" at breathless speed, he speaks the ensuing lines "I will not live without it" and "I perish on the spot" as no other Ko-Ko in my experience - he appreciates their witty double-entendre - and then, having convulsed the audience with laughter, he sang "Tit Willow" with extreme tenderness and sincerity.

Sir Ruthven Murgatroyd is no easy part - indeed, it is really two roles. Shy and conceited in Act I, good and modest in Act II, there was always a cheeky "Yes, uncle" at the end!

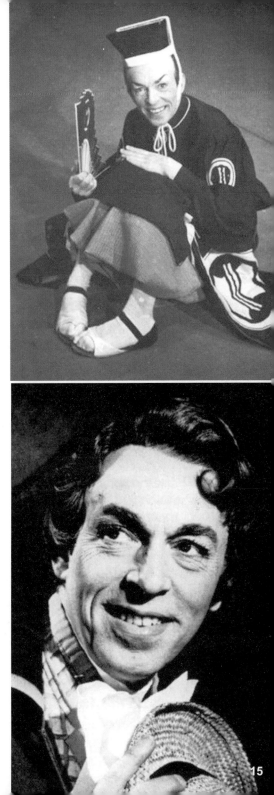

Jack Point will, I think, always be my favourite John Reed part, although "The Yeomen of The Guard" is not my favourite opera: the "Hamlet" of Gilbert and Sullivan roles, said Reed in a chat-show interview.

It is not always realised Jack Point has only five scenes in the opera, two of them very brief. Reed took these skilfully to show the change in Point's fortunes. His Point is not engaged to Elsie, but he regrets this omission, as soon as she marries the unknown prisoner. He knows his jokes to the Lieutenant are not too funny. Melancholy when reading Hugh Ambrose, ironic as he sings to Wilfred Shadbolt with all his customary clarity of diction and irony, unashamed in the "shot" scene (for which he adopted a paler make-up), you could see his suffering in Fairfax's wooing of Elsie and in his exquisitely tender "When a jester is outwitted". And those final moments, as he pathetically tries to recapture Elsie's affections which he never really held - and then with a half-laugh he has a fatal heart attack. A small point, but when Reed fell, he knew how to roll over half the stage and send a shiver up the spines of his audience.

In "The Gondoliers", by contrast, the **Duke of Plaza-Toro** is vocally immediately martial, elegant, stylish, and abounding in Gilbertian inner-humour.
A courtier grave and serious, indeed, whose dancing skill reminded one yet again that Reed is a dancer on the stage of very great ability. Burlesque ballet steps exaggerated, yes, but not to inartistic limits.

Fortunately, he has recorded for Decca all his roles, some more than once. Memories can be refreshed by playing records at home when one can recall his nuances of expression. It is for this reason that this appreciation has concentrated less on his considerable musicianship and more on his personality as an actor. The two, nevertheless, go together. If unexpected joie de vivre breaks out at a London "Last Night" (as when in 1979 his Bunthorne had 'Barclays" tattooed on his chest), he has never forgotten that Gilbert and Sullivan are humorists of word and note, and he has been a great interpreter of both. For nearly three decades of giving pleasure, one can say quite simply:
Thank you, John.

Chapter 1

"I PLY MY CRAFT AND KNOW NO FEAR"

The Ones That I Like

(John Reed talks to John Watt about his Favourite Parts)

John, I saw you quoted in a newspaper recently as saying that Jack Point was one of your favourite G. & S. parts:

Yes, well Jack Point has always been the one that I've kept a little apart from the others-partly because he was so entirely different and partly because of the different problems of characterisation.

But really when people say what is your favourite opera, I don't put that in amongst them at all. It's the one apart, and I leave that out thinking, well, maybe it is my favourite - but I don't think it is in point of fact. I only like parts of it. I like the serious parts of Jack Point.

You know, the last scene. It's rather like anybody who can make people laugh also wanting to know that he's got the ability to make them cry as well. Really it proves that you can act in it I suppose.

But I think that my favourite part has always been Ko-Ko, because it's such fun to do and you know that you're getting all the reaction that you want from them, and you make people laugh, and the children and everybody enjoy him. And I suppose that's what our job is here anyway. To entertain people.

Do you think it is public reaction that makes it for you?

Yes, I do. That's what colours it for me anyway. Of course we do so many of them it's very nice suddenly to have a change and do "Patience" which is a very great favourite of mine. I think that's perhaps because I don't do Bunthorne as much as I do Ko-Ko. If I did as many Patiences as I do Ko-Ko, I think perhaps I would choose Ko-Ko as being my favourite between the two.

Now the other parts, like the older parts, are the ones that when I first took over I had to work harder on, because they were so non-me, you see. Clearly, anybody further removed from people like Sir Joseph Porter, for instance, there just isn't . . .I hope! He's a snob and he's always correct and I'm quite the reverse. So I had to work on those and I believe they turn out to be my best parts because of that. Or I've grown old into them or something like that . . . maybe that's it!

Quite honestly, my juveniles now, I call them my character make-ups!

Which others in the older range of characters would you pick out?

I'm very fond of the Duke of Plaza-Toro now that it's been re-done by Anthony Besch - I prefer the new Duke to the old one. It all knits together much better really.

As an artist, which side of the characters you play appeals to you yourself most?

I like anything where the dancing comes in. I must say that, because however I worry about words and music - as anybody can - I never ever worry about the dancing.

I mean, I could fall flat on my bottom and it wouldn't bother me at all. But I can miss a word and I'm upset.

For instance, since I've started, I've never particularly liked those speeches that I have to say to her in "Pinafore" . . . things like

"Madam, it has been represented to me that you are appalled by my exalted rank. I desire to convey to you officially my assurance that if your hesitation is attributable to that circumstance, it is uncalled for." . . . it's so non-me. And once I get that out I think... that's that over, I could easily have messed that up. But when they start to dance-and it goes on much longer than anything else that goes before - I have no more worries. None at all. I think when I'm reincarnated I'm coming back as a dancer!

What are your favourite dancing parts then?

Well, it's not what I'd call real dancing - it's more movement. But I suppose the new "arrangement" rather than "dancing" in "The Sorcerer" . . . maybe because it's new I like "The Sorcerer."

Now that you've 'run-in' John Wellington Wells, what do you think about him?

Oh, I like him very much - I'm not finished with him yet, by any means. It's just beginning to form. As I've said before, when I first got the costumes that I wear, when you first take over, they're not yours. They don't belong to you. And, in fact, they are exactly the same costumes, some of them, as I got in the first place - and now I fit them. Now they belong to me. Now I put them on like I put on my own suit.

How long do you reckon it would take you to get right into a part?

Oh, quite a number of years. Because now, I've said before, if anything comes undone on the stage like a little button here, I can put it right without even looking down. It's like your own trousers or your own jacket. You would know exactly where that button was. It now belongs to you and so I think that your costumes almost fit round you like the characters do. I should say that as soon as - you say how long does it take - well, as soon as the character adjusts itself correctly, then so does the costume with it. It's almost as if when you get the costumes right then the character is right.

Do you remember which was the first character you got right out of all the principal roles you've played?

I don't think I've got any of them quite right yet! One works and each time I shudder to think what I was like last year compared to what I am this year. Maybe no different at all but one feels one's getting a bit better with it. This is why I'm always so ready when, as with the Duke, there is any new work we can do on the parts to re-characterise them. It makes us very happy to work on them.

Which was the one you were happiest with in 'breaking-in', then?

That's a very difficult question, for when you first take them over there's such a lot to do. It's not just like doing Ko-Ko for a whole month. You do Ko-Ko one night and something else the next night, and because of that it takes longer. But I think Ko-Ko must be the one that fitted into place first because Ko-Ko is almost me. There's a lot of me in the character. It lets me bring out my sense of humour and delivery of lines. It allows that.

John Reed

*It's closest to your own
character, you feel?*

Yes, I do. I reckon that one
person can play a part equally
as well as another but in a
different sort of way. I think
that Peter Pratt, for instance,
played Ko-Ko as a soulful little
fellow-timid, frightfully shy.
But mine's cheeky, I think.

It doesn't mean that it was any
the less good for being the way
that Peter played it. It suited
him better - but I couldn't play
it as Peter played it.

But this couldn't apply to the character parts because there's no doubt
about it that you must get your own personality through. Nevertheless,
Sir Joseph Porter is a snob anyway, and there's not so many ways to
play a snob but just be a snob and curl up your lip or whatever.
There's a bigger variety in what you can do with a part like Ko-Ko.

He could be an old man, a fat man, a young man-he's ageless as far as
I'm concerned, Ko-Ko. Whereas there is a set age almost for these other
older parts - well, round about. But a person like Ko-Ko to me is just
any age.

*John Wellington Wells, of course, is the great extrovert character,
isn't he?*

I think I like these sort of parts. If I am playing it in Cockney, I try but it
needs more acting than you would if you're just going to use your
normal voice. You're going to have to bring out something different. I
don't have to do that as Ko-Ko. I just play Ko-Ko as I speak normally,
only project it. But I've got to change my voice if I'm going to play a
part like the First Lord.

If I play Gama. I've got to crack my voice and be acid. Now the same
applies to the Sorcerer where I've got to put on a Cockney voice.

You mention King Gama-can we discuss him?

Well, when I first played Gama, I don't know whether it was said in so many words, but it seemed that I made him too nice - the wig was nice and clean and everything else like that - and I think the company and Miss Carte thought I was much too nice for Gama. Really because I felt sorry for poor old Gama. As is me, I felt sorry for this little old man who's got a hump on his back and so I had so much sympathy with him. But since I wasn't laying it on thick enough I said OK, so here goes, if that's the way you want it I can do it that way. And maybe I went too far. I don't know. But now I get what I call my Gama throat after I've finished playing it. And now I can't play it any other way. People might say, well, don't lay it on so thick - but I can't. I have to crack and scream and screech or whatever. But they asked for that anyway, so if it's too much for them I have to say you asked for it and you got it. They dirtied the wig down and a few things like this, and I went to town on it.

We haven't spoken about the Lord Chancellor at all yet, have we?

The Lord Chancellor's nice . . . I like him very much actually, although I often wish he didn't have the Nightmare Song because it's a bit of a marathon isn't it, really, when you think about it. And one knows it so well that one begins not to know it almost, and this is what you've got to watch. After singing it as many times as I have it begins coming out parrot-fashion, and in the middle of the song you can pull yourself up and say to yourself "What am I talking about? Have I sung that bit?"

Mind you, I don't think that song, that particular song, is as bad as some of the others. For instance, in the Major-General's Song, which is a lot of gibberish, anyway, a lot of disconnected things following one another. If you analyse the Nightmare Song, it does follow through. There's some continuity there. You know - "You're a regular wreck, with a crick in yer neck" and it all follows through like 'And you dream you are crossing the Channel and tossing about in a steamer from Harwich, which is something between a large bathing machine . . . and you're giving a treat. . ." It's a story being told.

*I remember you telling me the story which you told on the Scottish
Television programme about G. & S. & D'Oyly Carte and the night you
couldn't get off that steamer from Harwich ?*

Yes, because I couldn't get that following word. "And you dream you are
crossing the channel and tossing about in a steamer from Harwich".
Instead of saying "which" I said "and". So you go on again. "And you
dream you are crossing the channel and tossing about in a steamer from
Harwich, And you dream you are crossing the channel and tossing about
in a steamer from Harwich And you dream . . ."

As soon as I found "which" I was off! But these are all the little traps you
can fall into. Once you've done it, once you've made any mistake on stage,
no matter how many years pass by, whenever you sing over that part you
think right back to the moment you made the mistake. I do anyway.
I know that as the First Lord I went out and sang "When at anchor here
I ride, My bosom smells with pride" instead of 'swells' - now that's only a
letter. But you see I have two now to choose from - "smell' and "swell' and
I never, ever, sing that song but in a flash I say "which one is it?" Pick the
right one or else you're dead as a duck. And it's always a curse to you.
If you've ever made a flop it's there, it's somewhere there settled down in
you, and so you guard it, all the time. And the more you play a thing like
the Nightmare Song, the more places you've got to guard. The more places
you've slipped up some time, and so you've got so many points to watch.

What about Robin Oakapple?

I like Robin Oakapple. I think maybe I'm a bit old for it now. And it's a
pity because I feel him. I feel I'm so fundamentally a young person - I am
a young person you know. I mean I'm older than the part I'm playing, for
instance, but I feel young. That's what's difficult about it. And that's what's
a bit sad about it that he'll have to go pretty soon.

I was just thinking today that perhaps it would be a good idea if I went
over all the parts again and changed one or two slightly - or if someone
would do it for me so that I could get a new slant on them maybe.
I'm always willing to do that. Rather like what they did with the Duke, and
certainly, not that I've played it before, with the Sorcerer, who was never
played as a Cockney. I think there might be a new way to do them all.

That's an interesting thought. But do you think that the fan's would accept that?

Yes, the fans would accept it. Certainly I think that you would have to educate the fans into accepting it. As an instance I remember when I was playing the Duke and they decided that they were going to change the colour of the wig and they gave me a red wig-a long red, curly wig. And when I came out of the stage door after wearing it for the first time - it was a new production and out of all the things that were new a girl fan I recognised stopped me and suddenly said : "I don't like the new wig." It had annoyed her. Now I played in that wig for about two years and they decided to bring it back to the smaller white wig. The first time I wore it, who should I meet again at the stage-door afterwards but this same girl. "Oh, I do miss the red wig," she said.

People go off about "The Gondoliers". I get letters saying: 'Please give us back the Duke we learned to love and adore' . . because of all the encores they used to have. But if they saw the old production now - if it was possible to bring it back next week - I'm quite sure they wouldn't like it as well as this production. It's the same sort of principle. None of us ever come up to the old ones - we're all doing the same job in fact as Henry Lytton, and Martyn Green, and Bertha Lewis and everybody else. But to the old ones we're not as good as they were. We never will be until we're dead and gone!

But if you could bring those operas back - I'm not saying they wouldn't adapt themselves immediately under these modern conditions - but if these productions were to come back, they would be 'hammy' and they would probably be laughed off the stage. Because we've moved so gradually - for all that we're saying the same lines, it's in a modern way. You've just merely to look at some of the old photographs and I think you can laugh and smile at some of the costumes that they used to have, and the make-up with their little rose-bud mouths.

That rather gives the lie to the theory that Gilbert's original stage directions must be followed at all times. I'm all for tampering with the directions, because I think that Gilbert's directions have dated just the same as anything else. His words and the music live on - and, of course, the great tradition of the D'Oyly Carte company, which has been handed down through the generations.

Introduction

For 50 Years John Reed has been a "household" name across the worldwide Gilbert and Sullivan community. It wasn't so much his left shoulder blade that people travelled miles to see it was his unique ability. The consummate performer. As a little boy my mother took me to see the D'Oyly Carte Opera Company. And for twenty years I feasted on their performances in general and on John Reed's characterisations in particular. I never dreamed that this man who could fill a theatre with laughter by the simple movement of his head would ultimately become a friend; stay in my home for a month each year as he directed my Savoyards Appreciation Society (West Yorkshire). I discovered what a wonderful cook he was. I became an insomniac as we sat up night after night as John recounted the most hilarious anecdotes of his time with the D'Oyly Carte. I never imagined that the one and only John Reed would actually perform with my amateur group – Ko-Ko, Sir Joseph, Bunthorne, and Jack Point in 1988, the Centenary Year of "Yeomen of the Guard." I believe this was his last full performance. John Reed did not take – he gave. He was a wonderful teacher. He taught with his hands, his body, his voice. He was as nimble of foot as any octogenarian you are ever likely to meet. His "superstar" status never turned his head. John always remembered his happy, happy roots – a small colliery village in the North of England.

I shall always be grateful to John Reed. It was his enthusiasm and encouragement that ultimately influenced our decision to begin the International Gilbert & Sullivan Festival in Buxton, Derbyshire – a Festival which has become the biggest celebration of Gilbert and Sullivan anywhere in the world, and which enjoyed the avid support of John Reed through to his death in February 2010, his 94th birthday.

Foreword

(Written by John Reed himself in 1993.)

I don't expect this to be any literary achievement, and nor do I hope to do anything other than to tell my story – the story of my life before joining the D'Oyly Carte Opera Company; memories of my time with the Company – and after, right up to this present day. I write because so many people have asked me to do so. Friends and the fans who have been so loyal to me, and were certainly, most loyal to the Company.

I am a lucky man. Generally my health has been good. My frustration is failing eyesight. What started as an autobiography will be a mix of autobiography and biography. I suppose having played the Duke of Plaza-Toro so many times it is firmly in my head that "one does not follow fashion – one leads it!"

Looking back over my life, I would have to say that if I had any ambition at all it was to make people laugh and be happy. What better opportunity did anyone ever have than I? The chance to perform all those perfect roles written by Gilbert and Sullivan, and the opportunity of playing them in the biggest and best theatres in England, America and other parts of the world. It was certainly a privilege to have all those years.

I would very much like to dedicate this effort of mine first to my family; then to all those loyal and faithful fans; to my D'Oyly Carte family and the glorious audiences we had and lastly to my guide, my guardian, my manager, doctor, confidant and above all true and trusting friend. I raise my glass and always shall say to Nicki – *"thank you friend."*

Chapter 2

"A LITTLE CHILD OF BEAUTY RARE, WITH MARVELLOUS EYES AND WONDROUS HAIR"

Why don't you write a book? You simply must put it all down.
So many times has this sort of thing been said to me that I finally began to think – perhaps I really should try? Where to start when you haven't written anything before?

I was born in a very small colliery village in the North of England – Close House, number 38. I always thought it was a most peculiar name for any village – but there you are. It is still there, a few miles from Bishop Auckland, County Durham.

My father was the butcher there and so had his father been before him. Grandfather Reed was also a Methodist Minister – a very fine honest man, much loved in the district. Straight and as sincere as they come. I believe that during the First World War a bomb was dropped in front of our house and shop, which formed a very small crater, which in the words of my mother "would have held a horse and cart".

All the windows in the house were blown out with the exception of my Grandfather's. He became almost a legend in his own time in that tiny village. Indeed every time the siren blew for another air raid many of the villagers would come along to our home to be near Grandad. He would simply go to bed as if nothing was in the least different with the words that "God would look after him" – and believe me, He did.

Don't think for one moment that he was a quiet man by any means. Another wonderful tale told to me by my mother was that one particular Sunday when he wasn't preaching himself, but sitting in the family pew, there was a very long-winded preacher taking the service. He was noted for taking an age over his sermon and the whole congregation knew it. Grandfather certainly knew it. The preacher announced the next hymn and said we would now sing hymn number 564 - 'Oh for a thousand tongues to sing.' My Grandfather said very loudly from his seat – "Nay lad, one like thine's plenty!"

Father didn't do any Chapel work as far as I can remember – but believe me he was equally as good a man in his own way. Just as much a character. I loved my parents dearly – still do, and can never bring myself to think that they are not still with me. I and my three sisters were brought up with pure love – as pure as it comes. I never saw or heard any arguments or the like at home. I had the most wonderful childhood and have nothing but the beautiful memories of that time.

So back to our home in Close House and the little window where the sun came peeping in at morn. This colliery village comprised only a few streets, six or seven shops including my Father's. Our shop had the house attached to it – sitting room, dining room, kitchen, long passages, a winding staircase with a banister rail, which I remember sliding down from top to bottom. It had a wonderful curve in the middle. A perfect slide and it was here I was born, February 13th during the First World War. I was christened John Lamb Reed. Naturally everyone thought my middle name Lamb was because my Father was a butcher – at least at school they did. In point of fact it was my Father's Father's Mother's maiden name. I quite like it now – but when I was younger I didn't care for it at all.

Grandfather Reed holds the reins. John's father is riding the horse.

My Grandfather was also called John Lamb Reed. I don't remember him at all. How I wish I had known him. I am told that on the day that I was born, which was a Sunday, he was on his way to Chapel. He was a Wesleyan Methodist Minister – not as Gilbert suggested "One of the most bigoted and persecuted types." Much the reverse, if I am to believe everything that was ever told to me about him. He was heading towards the Chapel when someone rushed to tell him that I had arrived. Children loved him and followed him everywhere. He always carried sweeties in his pockets. When he heard the news he fell to his knees in the middle of the street with a prayer of thanks and relief. I am told I was the apple of his eye.

I am also told that when he was in the pulpit it was nothing for him to talk to the congregation saying things like " come along Mrs Jones - you can do better than that. Let us hear you all raise your voice to God"

Close House. What a perfect playground for a child my home turned out to be.

My dad's nickname was "Pop" for the simple reason that he would always be saying " just pop upstairs for my glasses honey" or "pop to the shop for a packet of Target" his favourite tobacco......." Just pop here or there"....... So "Pop" he became. A wonderful devoted parent. Being the youngest and only boy I used to get away with so much. Sister Anne was four years older than I – whilst Chris and Betty were like two extra mothers just caring for and protecting me.

At certain times of the year when the fancy took me I would hold a fair with Mother's approval and assistance. She would bake all sorts of little fancy cakes and goodies and allow me to cover a huge clothes horse with sheets making a large tent for fortune telling or any other game which came to mind. There was also the aerial flight. For the price of a pin you could climb to the top of a wall at the far end of the yard on a ladder, and from the top of the wall I would have strewn a rope down to the other side of the yard floor. Up you could go with a hooked walking stick, hang it over the rope and then hang on for dear life and glide to the ground at the other end of the yard. All for the price of one pin. Why a pin, absolutely escapes me – but there again I never did have any business sense. For another pin you could crawl into a large barrel at the top of the yard and be rolled to the bottom. Very uncomfortable. One pin for that! Looking back it was overcharging and not very popular either.

I spent a lot of time preparing a shower. Somewhere I had found an old zinc bath and with the aid of hammer and nail I pierced dozens of holes in the bath. This was then tied somehow to the top of the ceiling in the "pot-house", secured well and I then stuck a hosepipe into the tin. For two pins, if you wished, after donning a bathing suit you could stand under the bath tin and be showered with very cold water. I took the pins but never entered into this frivolity although it proved highly popular in the warmer weather.

The highlight of my "fair" was without doubt the "sky rides." People came miles to see it! At the top of the archway, Pop had a block and tackle fixed which had many uses, which I will talk about later. For several pins - it was the most expensive attraction - you could sit in a leather hoop attached to this contraption and be pulled to the ceiling.

It was quite cheap at the price and there was usually a queue for this ride. Hannah Ingledew, younger sister of Beatrice was the last in the queue one day. She paid her pins and was duly pulled to the ceiling and tied off for her spell. I was distracted with some other task and then mother called me for lunch. Everyone else had gone off for their meal. I clean forgot about Hannah who remained tied to the ceiling until the fair resumed after lunch. She never came to the fair again! She was older than most of my friends and certainly too big for the barrel.

There were of course other games of less importance but Mother's tea was the highlight of the afternoon and what is more important, unlike me she did not charge. What I did with a lapel full of pins I cannot imagine. The only benefit I can think of would be for Mother's dressmaking. She certainly was an excellent dressmaker.

There were always animals around the house – dogs, calves, piglets – and I always had some kind of pet. Prior to my arrival the dogs were working creatures or guard dogs kept in kennels. However I was allowed to have my own pet - even a pet lamb. I think it got a bit much with "Billy" who was a pet pig trying to get through the back door when quite large.

Chapter 3

"WHEN I WAS A LAD"

Early Life

Close House consists of two long streets running to Eldon Lane and Cownden. I was actually born in my parents' home. The house seemed big to me as a child. The rooms were large and many. My Father had a huge slaughterhouse by the side, leading to stables for animals – cows, sheep and horses. There was a huge yard and a pothouse used for Father's business – making sausages, polonys, potted meat and the like.

John loved the animals - particularly as seen here on horseback

To me it was an exciting adventure land. The loft above the stables. The straw. The hiding places. The machine for cutting turnips to feed the cattle: the large wooden bins holding cow-cake; the smell of it all – yes I still know that smell.

John's parents

All this and a wonderful family too. A perfect Mother and Father who loved me along with my three older sisters. Being the youngest and the only boy they all spoiled me, except perhaps Anne who was too near my own age.

It did not seem remotely unusual that all of us sang and played the piano – or spent night after night around the piano entertaining ourselves and most likely relations or friends. Ours was always an open house and whoever called was always invited to come in and have a cup of tea, which of course meant the cakes, always home-made, especially at Christmas, with some Christmas cake, a piece of rice cake and a slice of cheese plus a small silver coin on the plate.

The choir from the Chapel would pass our house when out Carol Singing and would return for the last Carols to us – everyone coming in and filling all the way up the staircase if there was no room left downstairs. The cake was there for all – plus ginger wine! Oh dear nothing intoxicating for Methodists! So what! We never needed it for everyone was having too good a time.

Mother would often be found singing at some choir weekend or something along with the other professional singers who had been brought from London. Hers was one of those voices, which I often think was not that of "just another soprano". She was Mrs Reed, with a quality that one so seldom hears right from the heart – heaven knows her heart was big enough.

One day after a concert, men arrived at the door of 38 Close House with a contraption to make a record of a song they had heard my Mother sing the night before. Records were very new in those days and quite unheard of in Close House. Father would not allow it. I really don't think that Mother minded – gosh I wish she had made that record. How I would love to hear that voice again.

And do you know the most awful thing of all is that I had my mother's voice recorded on tape. My sister was shy of that tape, but not my mother. She sang, she did everything on it. I was burgled in London and they took my tape recorder and all my tapes. It's very strange. When I came back from America I had bought a new 3D camera and I took all these photographs of my mother. I had bought her all these broaches, and she put them all on at once and said 'oh my heavens, I look like Woolworths'. Not one of those pictures came out. All the rest did - but nothing with my mother on. When I got back from my next tour the Police came to tell me my mother had died. The home broke up after her death, and my sisters said "John you must have this suite, you must have this bedroom suite." I said "I don't want anything. There's one thing I do want. I want my mother's rolling pin!" And I have it to this day, and I make pastry, and I put my hands on this rolling pin and it's my mother's hands on there. It's the only thing I have of my mother's.

My youngest sister, four years my senior, became a schoolteacher and
eventually married a Minister – Methodist of course. Betty, the middle
one was a brilliant pianist but preferred to be called an organist.
In fact she had her first position as organist around the age of 14.
To me she was the best accompanist ever. Of course I suppose I would
say that wouldn't I? She was my sister.

Christina, the eldest, was a housewife with a wonderful husband, as
indeed they all had. We lost Chris before my last tour of America.
I was actually playing in Nottingham and had to rush up to the funeral
and immediately back to Nottingham to prepare for going to the States.
Strange, I was so busy with that tour and taken up with the travelling it
was not until I returned five or six months later that I cried and broke
my heart again. I think it was when I realised that this time I had only
two presents to bring back home from my travels. It always delighted me
to come back with cardigans, dresses, jewellery or whatever else
I thought would be different from things that they would be able to buy
for themselves here.

I think, like my Mother, I have always been clever with my hands.
I could turn them to anything. This was unlike my Father who only
knew his own job.

I well remember the day he came in when Mother had decided to freshen
up the ceiling with a new coat of whitewash – or emulsion paint in those
days. It was an old saying "Belamy whitewash, any colour you like."
She intended to do it very carefully, and not to splash the wallpaper.
She was almost finished with only two square yards to complete the job,
when in came Pop. "What are you doing up there Honey
(He called us all Honey) you will kill yourself."

"I am alright Bob" she said.

"Come down" he replied. "I will finish it for you." Famous last words!!

Down she came as he bade, and up went Father. After a stroke or two
with the brush he said – "By Jove this is hard work Honey" and
immediately dropped the brush, placed the bucket with the remaining

whitewash on a shelf, went down to retrieve the brush, started to mount the steps again but bumped the bucket with his head, upset it over his head and the whitewash was everywhere. It ruined the wallpaper and he was covered completely, head to foot with the stuff. I thought my Mother would die laughing. Father too. That was how it went. There were no cross words, only a huge joke to be spoken of many, many times. That was my happy family. He was a man who could slaughter a beast, twist a chicken's neck or what ever was needed for his profession – but would not hurt a fly and who would drop a tear when any of us left home for any short time – even a holiday. He would stand silently at the bottom of the bed concerned and anxious when any of his children were slightly off colour.

Mother told me that once when I was very small I had been taken to bed by her and had to kneel by the side of the bed and say my prayers. "God Bless Grandma, Christina, Betty and Anne. Make me a good boy..." Well this particular night I had said all those things and added strictly off my own bat if you will pardon the expression "Please God send me a tennis racket." Mother had of course come down the stairs, smiling no doubt and saying – "what do you think he's said tonight?" Father was told about the tennis racket. Without a word to anyone he got up, put on his cap – he loved his cap did Pop – and left the house. He went to the side door of a shop (it was after closing time) and I woke the following morning to find a tennis racket on my bed. Could anyone ever have had a better dad than that?

When I was much older – seventeen or so and driving a car and going to dances which often went on until 2 o'clock in the morning my father used to tell me it was much too late for me to be out. It seems funny now. I would say to Mother I'm going to such and such a dance; can I take the car? She would say – of course, just tell your Father. I would go and tell him and he would say, "you will kill yourself going to these dances." I would tell my Mother that he didn't want me to go and she would say, "take no notice of that. Don't be silly just get yourself ready." I would and sure enough there was the car already out of the garage, washed, with Father rubbing it over with a final polish. "Drive carefully and take care" he would grin. So it was this sort of treatment that made all of us never ever do anything to hurt them or upset them. I sometimes believe that Father was the original beatnik – in the nicest way of course. He loved a piece of silk, any silk around his neck. I well remember one of my sisters looking for a pair of silk stockings for instance, she found one – the other was round his neck. "Oh sorry Honey" he said. He had never even thought he was doing anything out of place. "Here's some money – go and buy yourself some more." No doubt for a further supply for him! Oh that dear loveable man.

Mother was so perfect for him. Truly a marriage made in Heaven. She cared for him, guided him. Indeed Father was a hopeless business man and would have given everything he had away especially if anyone came with a tale of woe, and at times that darling Mother of mine had to appear hard for she was our real protector – and his too.

In those days we had perhaps the very first car in the area – a twenty-four or twenty-five horse powered Ford. It was something I have never heard of before or since. It was a butcher's van, which could be unbolted from the chassis and the van part pulled along and up to the ceiling by block and tackle. Then you could lower down onto the chassis a towing part, which when duly bolted down converted it to a family car, in which we were able to spend our free time at weekends. The seaside was only twenty miles away and we loved to go there.

During the outings, perhaps travelling at twenty-five miles an hour, which was really moving in those days, Mother would say – "blow your horn Bob. Blow your horn."

"I am alright Lizzie–Anne" he would say. He always called her Lizzie-Anne. I can never understand why with a lovely name like Elizabeth Anne, but there you are. Well Bob would never do her bidding and blow the horn. So Mother who was always frequenting sales, bought her own horn. A large brass thing with a twist before you got to a large rubber end. From that day she would sit with it on her knee during our outings and hang it out of the window and blow it whenever she felt it was needed, in spite of Father's protestations. Characters they certainly were.

Can you not just see the sight of the family, driving along in the van? During a busy time, when Father had no time to put on the touring part, my sisters and I would sit in armchairs in the back, with a piece of meat gauze between us and our parents and only small pieces of the same gauze round the van, which obscured us from the passers by. And there was Mother poking that funny old horn out of the window and blasting away at every opportunity. At the same time an unearthly din of some popular tune coming from us in the back, singing at the top of our voices, with Mother joining in and Father whistling or grunting at the same time, which in itself was quite an achievement. What our neighbours must have thought! What glorious times they were. Our large old house had high ceilings and one of the bedrooms was a playroom. It contained a large doll's house, which opened at the front revealing all the furniture. I can remember papering that house out with wallpaper left over from Mother's decorating. The large patterns had not been made for a doll's house and consequently we would end up with a bedroom with a wall covered with one solitary rose. There was a rocking horse too, which was covered with real horsehide.

I spent many hours playing at 'Post Offices' with my cousin Nancy. We would never speak a word. I had concocted cotton all over the room to which had been threaded wooden bobbins, which could carry a written message attached to it to any part of the room. This of course also served for playing shops. You know "change Miss Witherspoon" like the old fashioned larger stores had for catapulting that cylindrical container to the store office for money change.

I suppose it was here that I first started my stage career. Eventually I built myself a stage, which was a very large table and of course there had to be a curtain to draw, which was supplied by Mother. She, Nancy and I then performed "The Princess and the Candlestick maker", all made up on the spur of the moment. Never ever twice alike, but oh how I believed it all.

Sometimes we would perform this in the sitting room, which had a bay window. This was excellent for a stage for it had heavy curtains to draw, which worked much better than the ones I had arranged in the playroom. Was it unusual, or do all children act this way? I suppose they do.

Life is always pretend at that age. It is just that I never grew up.
I suppose I had to continue acting. I had my music lessons with
Mr Dakin, who used to come to the house. He had already taught my
sister Betty, until she outplayed him – but he did not have the same
success with any other member of the family. All of us played a little.
Both Chris and Anne could manage to thump out a hymn quite well,
like myself I suppose, but I was the only boy in the family and quite
spoiled by both Father and Mother, to say nothing of my older sisters.
By the time Mr Dakin got to me he was getting much older and would
drop off to sleep while I was struggling with "Blackberry Waltz" or the
"The Fair Dance" with the family portraits jumping about on top of the
piano. One day he woke with a start because I hit a wrong note.
He took my hand and banged it on the right note. I did no more than
get up from my seat, remove my music, went to my Mother and said,
"I am not going in there anymore." She went in to see what exactly had
happened. Mr Dakin had popped off to sleep again, what really
happened I do not know. Or what was said. But I never had Mr Dakin
again, although eventually I went to a lady down the street – Miss
Peacock. The poor dear had no success with me either, but at least I had
that foundation and it helped when eventually I had to teach myself a
song or especially to bang out my own part from a trio or quartet.

Such was the freedom I had as a young boy, that any friend I made,
or indeed my sister's friends too, were immediately brought home on
the very first meeting. I am sure now that this was Mother's idea of
keeping an eye on the type of people we were associating with.
Consequently there were always the parties both inside and out in a
massive yard as it seems to be now. The arched covered part ran at
right angles to the yard and the full width of the house. This was
where the car was adjusted by block and tackle. Such an excellent
place for children to play.

I started school at Eldon, which was only ten minutes walk from my
home. Usually it was my sister Betty who had the job of taking or
dragging me there – for I hated it. I was such a hopelessly shy child.
When I was a little older I was transferred to another school,

merely I think because I was not clever – but older. I can't remember its name, but it was there I sat my scholarship for the grammar school in Bishop Auckland. As I recall it was quite something to go to the grammar school. I passed my examination. Heaven knows how or why, but what is more I passed at a high level. It was as I remember then, if one passed at a certain level you were accepted free. At another level you paid a certain amount towards your education. The lower level meant your parents had to pay the whole amount or you failed entirely. Being a very sensitive creature, I recall I became very upset at the beginning of the term to be one of the only boys who did not go out to the teacher with an envelope containing the necessary fee. I have always been so very independent and remember asking my Mother why I could not take some money like the other boys. I thought I was receiving charity, which was not at all the case, for we were always very comfortably off. She explained the whole thing to me. So perhaps I was a little brighter than ever I thought I was.

Off I went to King James Grammar School. I was beginning to enjoy it by this time, and there I remained until the family moved to Darlington. I must have been about eleven years old by this time. We were moved to Darlington because there had been the miners strike in the collieries and Father being a butcher had drawn all the money he had to buy cattle to slaughter. Yes he slaughtered the beasts himself. It was long before abattoirs you must remember. The strike went on a very long time and Father's money slowly but surly disappeared until we were almost bankrupt. He fed so many of those miners on the understanding that they would pay him back when the strike was over.

Well the strike was over and Father had huge debts. Instead of paying him back many of those miners took their business elsewhere. This broke his heart and he had a complete breakdown. Carefully tended by his darling wife and his devoted family, he recovered, but Mother insisted that the next business we took would be with the money actually coming over the counter. She and only she was responsible for our move to a Darlington fish and chip shop, which was at that time doing no business at all. Not for long, I may add. At the beginning Mother had all of us going up and down the streets around the new shop with bills saying – "Fish shop at number 10 Mayfair Road, under New Management." So keen we were to help the situation I am sure that both my sisters and myself saw to it that no house was missed out. I used to fry the fish - and I rather liked it. The business gradually grew and grew. Mother was most definitely the business one of our little family.

John - the would - be golfer; above, at home in Darlington; and to the right with his fire service colleagues.

Chapter 4

"LIFE IS A JOKE THAT'S JUST BEGUN"

I can divide my life roughly into three parts – or three large families. First there was my really true family, of which I have told you a little part and the family around me during the war period, when I was away from my real home in Darlington; second the largest family of all of them – the D'Oyly Carte family of 28 years; and finally my family since retiring from the D'Oyly Carte.

The war years were really happy ones at the beginning. I was still in Darlington and somehow found myself in the Auxiliary Fire Service – always on call in case of an air raid warning.

Many was the night I was called out of bed, pulled clothes on top of pyjamas, jumped into the car and drove quickly to my station, attached a pump to the back of the fire tender, picked up the other Firemen and stood by waiting for whatever attack came. There were a few incendiary bombs we put out but nothing more than that.

Once in Richmond, Yorkshire, (I was working in an Insurance Office at that time and still doing my Fire Service) I had to drive a huge Fire Engine with all the Firemen on board outside of the town. It was a small road and as I was driving up a hill the air raid siren blew, which meant we had to return…. and quick. I had to turn that great big engine around in that narrow lane. I only succeeded in getting the thing stuck across the road with the exhaust jammed in the mud and exploding like mad. Thank God we were not needed. Just as well - I had made my own private war up there in the Richmond hills complete with sound effect.

Really I did very little in the Fire Service, with perhaps the exception of fire watching duty.

Other friends of mine had gone either into the Army or the Airforce long before my age group came up. When it did I volunteered for the Airforce. I was going to be a Pilot. Nothing less…..but no, I did not even pass the medical. I was mortified. The paper said I had a slight trace of sugar in my bloodstream. I was taken poste-haste to the family doctor who said is was so slight that it had probably been caused by "emotional excitement".

I was a member of Darlington Operatic Society and played many of the comic roles. And I just loved my dancing. We used to do Cabarets all over the North East , for big balls and dances. Joy Bidell, was my most regular partner. She's in New Zealand now. We used to put on quite a show. So dancing was then and always has been easy for me. I did ballroom dancing and got all my medals. Victor Sylvester. Quick, quick slow. I got all the medals for that, but that doesn't help much in Gilbert and Sullivan. You don't quickstep round the stage when you're playing Jack Point - but it did of course teach you to move.

Ballet dancing - 'The dream of Olwen" at The Hipperdrome

When eventually I was really called up and had to go for another medical, I passed A1 but when they discovered the earlier results they failed me yet again. I could not stand the fact that I was doing nothing towards the war effort and my next move was to become an instrument worker at Letchworth in Hertfordshire. I billeted myself with a charming family, Mr & Mrs Slade and I remember becoming very friendly with Lillian, who worked in a Ladies Outfitters. We used to go dancing an awful lot and I decided to continue with my ballroom dancing lessons, which I had begun in Darlington at the Winifred Boylan Dancing School. I continued until I had all my medals. These were all pointers to my ultimately taking to the stage, though indeed at that time nothing was further from my mind.

Meantime I continued my war effort as an instrument worker and was very proud to be able to work to 2/10th of a thousand part of an inch. I think I was very good at that job.

"New Moon" with Darlington Operatic Society, and other roles with the Kay Players and Keith James Repertory Company.

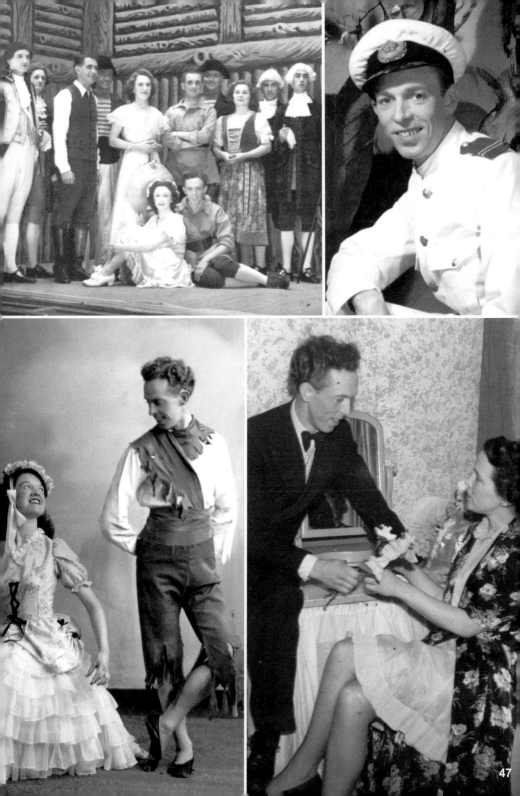

The war was drawing to an end and I tried desperately to get my release to return North. Finally I was permitted to leave, but had to take a job in another factory up there. Once home and settled with my family again I met Marjorie – a member of the Kay Players Dramatic Society. I had previously had elocution lessons from Miss Smithson who lived in Stockton, a town close to Darlington, and had also done a small part or two in the Darlington Operatic Society.

This particular night the Kay players were reading "Goodness How Sad" a play by Robert Morley. They asked me to read in the part of the leading man – an actor and Film Star. I did and they liked it and after some persuasion got me to say that I would play the role. Oh yes I remember that part. I had to smoke a cigar continuously when I was on stage. I swear I was green after every performance.

The Kay players were named after their founder Mrs Kay Barrow, who was a hard taskmaster but always a great help to all of us. We did many plays. Strange how one thing always led to another.

One day a gentleman came to the door of my home to ask if I would contemplate playing juvenile parts in his repertory company in Stockton – Keith James Enterprises. I said – "but you don't know what I can do."

He said, " I've seen you make an entrance and an exit. That's good enough for me." I thought he must be out of his mind and certainly didn't know what on earth he meant. I do now. The most important thing for any actor is to hit the audience on arrival.

So I started an acting career. I did everything in that Company. And not just the juvenile parts. I painted the set. And if I only had a small part I would often prompt. I found it very easy to learn the lines – sometimes six or even seven hundred speeches a week. As we were presenting one play one week we were waiting for the next week's play to arrive to see just how much we had to learn. I remember one Thursday the following week's play arrived and my name went up on the board to play Nigel in "Love in a Mist" – a whacking part, hardly ever off the stage for the whole night. After the performance I drove home as quickly as I could to get something to eat and sit up until I had at least got the first act under my belt stop. After all we were to play it on the Monday.

When I did get home Mother and Father were still up and mother was telling Father all the happenings of the day. Perhaps I forgot to mention Father was slightly hard of hearing. It had happened when he was young – water in the ear when swimming. Wherever I went in the house I could usually hear Mother with raised voice relating just what she had done during the day.

I decided to have a bath and they would then have decided to retire and I could get down to studying the part. I went up the first flight of stairs to the bathroom, turned on the hot water and put my old tattered copy of the play on the edge of the bath.

I returned to the bathroom a few minutes later to discover to my horror that the book had slipped into the hot soapy water. This particular copy of the play must have been around every repertory company in the theatre for every page was loose and floating. I was horrified. There was so little time before we were to perform the wretched thing. What to do? As it happened my folks had retired, so I put on the electric iron and pressed every sheet dry, and then sat up through the night. I had the first act memorised by the rehearsal on Friday morning and the play went on as usual on Monday.

My time in the repertory theatre was very exciting. After all it was my first experience of working on stage professionally. Keith James had taken great pains to recommend that I should not tell the rest of the company that this was the first professional company I had been in.

"They don't like amateurs" he said. "You see they are put out of the theatre and are out of work when the amateurs take over the theatre for their annual shows." This had never even occurred to me before. So my entry into the Keith James Repertory Theatre Company was with my lips sealed. Occasionally when the play for the week had a larger cast than Keith had, he would draw from the local amateurs the best they had to offer. They came willingly enjoying both the experience and the opportunity.

Often some member of the regular company would say something like "it's not right bringing these amateurs in." I remained with my lips still sealed of course for indeed many of the interlopers were most probably far superior to myself.

It was quite hard work but I never noticed. I was loving it. Learning lines was no chore to me for I had it seemed a photographic memory. When I dried, when rehearsing I could half close my eyes and see the printed words and the position on the page.

Chapter 5

"IF YOU'RE ANXIOUS FOR TO SHINE"

The D'Oyly Carte

I became a member of the D'Oyly Carte Opera Company in the year 1951. It all started through a casual meeting in the street. I remember I had just got off the trolley bus from town and was strolling home when I met Ron Thornton, whose brother Eric was a principle in the D'Oyly Carte. Eric and I had been in a show together some time before with the Darlington Operatic Company. The show was "The Duchess of Danzig."
I remember the title but little else about that particular musical except that I had to dance a lot in it and the part of Papillon had a distinct similarity to Jack Point. Napoleon and a washerwoman were also in the play somewhere and I can see Eric in a Soldier's Uniform. I knew very little about Ron and don't think I ever saw him again from that day to this.

Certainly he caught my interest talking about spiritualism of which he was a great believer, and in the course of the conversation said that his brother Eric had been on a visit and had been discussing his position with the D'Oyly Carte and the fact that the company were looking for someone to understudy the principle comedy role. Eric had said that he could only think of one person who might be satisfactory – and that was me. I suppose he was remembering our performing together in the show and my portrayal of Papillon.

He wondered if I would be interested. I subsequently heard from Eric that I was expected to attend auditions in Glasgow and I was to learn "The Nightmare Song" from Iolanthe. I thought little of learning the song. After all I was learning a play a week for the repertory company. At that time I knew little of Gilbert and Sullivan and even less about the D'Oyly Carte Opera Company – my education in that field had been sadly neglected. Little did I know how very quickly this would be corrected.

So off I went by train to Glasgow. Everything was quite rushed. Armed with the music of Iolanthe and one or two other songs, I arrived at the Hotel where the auditions were taking place. I remember many others were in the same boat as myself and after seeing so many applicants thought what little chance of any success I might have. I wanted the audition over so as not to waste their precious time on me. They heard me first.

Was I nervous? I don't recall, but knowing myself I must have been. The second song that I sang was "Jack's the Boy" from "The Country Girl." The whole audition only took minutes and I remained long enough to hear someone say "Thank you Mr Reed, we'll let you know."

That's that I thought, I won't hear any more from them. Once out of the torture chamber and feeling free I decided to book into the best hotel I could find and make a night of it by booking to see a show before returning home the following morning. I wasn't really interested in watching the D'Oyly Carte. I booked for the ballet.

I had been home about a week when I heard from the company asking me to audition yet again in front of Miss Bridget D'Oyly Carte who would be with them in Edinburgh where they had moved on their tour. The journey was harrowing. The taxi, which was ordered, to take me to the station was late and I only just caught the train, but in spite of that and other irritating things I was there on time at the theatre.

This time it was much different. The crowd of "opponents" were thinned down to three or so and this time we were in a theatre. I have always felt much more at home in these surroundings.

So out I went onto the rather darkened stage, unable to see if anyone at all was in the auditorium. I sang my songs as before in the same order and a voice from the darkness asked me to do some dialogue. I obliged with a "mad and long speech" from a play I had done recently from Berkeley Square in which I charge round the stage threatening, screaming and calling all my invisible acting members "ghosts! ghosts! you are all ghosts."

When I finally stopped, there was a deadly hush. "Oh dear" I thought, "you have gone too far this time John."

Then the voice from the darkness again – "We want you Mr Reed. How soon can you join us."

I staggered into the wings from the stage and already there was Mr Lloyd who I learned afterwards was the company general manager. I must have said that I would need at least nine weeks to finish up all sorts of things I was engaged in. He gave me four or five of the operas to study and I left the theatre by the stage door in a total and complete daze. I stayed the night again in the best Hotel I could find in Edinburgh and went to the theatre – this time to see "The Gondoliers" performed by the D'Oyly Carte Opera Company. It was the first time I had ever seen them.

The day I returned home the phone rang; it was the Company to ask if, since they were to move on to Newcastle the following week, which was only 30 miles or so from my home town, I possibly could join them there in another week's time. In a weak moment I said, "yes, perhaps I could." I learned to be very grateful for that weak moment. It was one mad dash around to clear everything up, but somehow I did it; and two weeks after my final audition I was a member of the D'Oyly Carte Opera Company.

Yes, that is how I became a member of the "family" (for that is what we were), my family for the next 28 years. It was an ever-changing and growing family, for once someone was in with them, if they left for whatever reason, they somehow still belonged and were forever coming back to visit.

Chapter 6

"HEAR ME, HEAR ME, IF YOU PLEASE, THESE ARE VERY STRANGE PROCEEDINGS"

Understudy

Ann Drummond Grant

Joyce Wright

As a new member of the D'Oyly Carte Opera Company I am quite sure my entrance into it was much different than others.

It was funny because I was kept apart from the rest of the company for most of the time, because they were teaching me all the understudy stuff that we had to do. And all I would do at night was walk up and down backstage. Everybody was looking at me wondering "who the dickens I was."

It was most amusing to hear the principals warming up with their exercises. Well I didn't know anything like that. I wasn't a trained singer. There was Ann Drummond Grant – "Drummie" to us and she was doing her warm ups - "ohohohohoh," and if anybody knocked at the door, she would change it to "ohohohowhatisitnowdear." It all ran into one. There was miniminime Joyce Wright miniminime, miniminime, miniminime. Later on everybody had these sort of exercises. One person used to stand by the

wall and go bah,bah,bah. Well I hadn't anything to do like that.
So I use to go oooo,oooo, any old thing. I really didn't know what it was
all about, and that's the honest truth. Singing was just an extension of
my speaking voice, that's all, which seemed to fit these parts beautifully.

My first week

So tell me about your first week or month with the D'Oyly Carte

'My first week in Newcastle was strange. I was kept like a thing apart.
No one knew me. I was wandering around the theatre and nobody
introduced me to anybody. I was just wandering around as they were
rehearsing me in the morning with all the parts because evidently the
understudy fellow that I was replacing was leaving in a month so I had
to learn the parts quickly. I had to learn them all.'

'So who would coach you through these then John?'

"Snookey" Evans coached me through all those early days, and dear
old Bill Cox-Ife did the music with me. What a wonderful man he was,
I owe a lot to him. So for the whole of that first month, I didn't meet
anybody. I didn't take my car with me. When it came to train calls,
I was sitting there and people were sort of looking at me, wondering
who I was.

I always remember waiting in a queue somewhere, somewhere a long
way from home. I was at the end of the queue, and I remember a taxi
stopping opposite me and a girl called Shirley Hall, who played Rose
Maybud – I remember a lovely Rose Maybud, the best I have ever
seen - shouted across 'would you like a lift John', and I said 'you are
an angel.' I've put her on a pedestal ever since.

And in among all this training I had to go on as chorus really before
I was ready. I knew the principal roles, but I was thrown into the chorus.
My first time on in the chorus I was flourishing my fan and the pin
came out at the bottom. By the time I was finished there was just all
this debris round my feet and me waving this bit of paper; I thought -
Oh God this is the end of the world; but of course nobody even saw me,
but it was terrible.'

'Someone once told me that being in the chorus of the D'Oyly Carte was like painting by numbers, was it like that, that you had a number?'

'Yes. Yes, I suppose it was, but it was more so with principals I should say, than it was with the chorus. With the chorus you moved in a mob. It was like two lines here with the ladies in front of you practically, although they have changed all that now – I helped them change is as a matter of fact. I remember going on with Ann Drummond Grant for instance. Peter Pratt was ill and I was rehearsing Bunthorne with her. She had gone over to stage left, I think. I was sitting on the stump at the side and said, 'I'll meet this fellow and beat him on his own ground' – I jumped up at her and she dried completely. She dried. I remember whoever was directing saying 'you should have stood on another word!' Because I didn't stand on the word that Peter Pratt stood on, it dried her completely.

That is what it was like. We knew it had to change. Of course as an understudy you'd actually have to do what the Principal does because you can't alter the whole thing. You have to do what you are asked to do, which I did quite willingly, but when I went on for myself, I went where I wanted to go and where I wanted to move because I can't be like anybody else. I never used to watch Peter from the wings because I didn't want to be a carbon copy of anybody.'

What was it like going on as understudy to Peter Pratt? What was the audience reaction?'

'Oh yes, I think it is difficult for anybody that takes over from someone who is established and have their own following and fans – but you have to win them over sooner or later. I was very fortunate as it didn't take me all that long, but of course I met up with it. There were two youths in the front that were fans of Peter's and when I came on they used to tut and look the other way. They actually looked back towards the audience and wouldn't look at me on the stage. It was as if I had been responsible for pushing Peter away. I didn't push Peter away. He left of his own accord. I didn't want his job either, I was happy in the chorus. I loved the chorus and I loved the people in the chorus, and I still do.

22nd May, 1952.

Dear Mr. Reed,

I was very pleased with the progress you have made, and, in view of the extra time you have put in on rehearsals, I have decided that, as from next week, your salary will be raised to £11:0:0d. per week.

I am informing Mr. Worsley of this to-day.

Yours sincerely,

Bridget D'Oyly Carte

Yes, it is not easy taking over, but I kind of soon won them over. I was lucky. I hope I had made some impression playing the Judge, Antonio, Annibale, the Major and Cox in Cox and Box. So whilst understudy for the leading roles I was playing some small parts and I also did chorus. When I started in 1951 I got £9.00 a week. After a year, I think, they gave me a £2.00 rise, I was understudying and I was playing these parts.'

'Was the D'Oyly Carte chorus a disciplined chorus?'

'Oh yes, I think they were disciplined. They had to be. Poor old Jimmy Marsland was an example of that you know. Over the years that chorus line, the semi-circle of men in Pirates for instance, had moved perhaps a yard further towards the front, but Jimmy was still standing in his old position. Every time I went round he used to say, 'they are all wrong you know, they should be back here, they should be back here.' If Jimmy had played one step forward, he would have put the whole thing right, but no, they were all wrong!

'So, how would you have described the D'Oyly Carte's policy on production?'

'Well, at that stage, I thought it was pretty marvellous really. It was all so schooled and everything else was so right and so well rehearsed. It wasn't until when I took over the roles and wanted to do things myself – you know, when it really mattered to me to be in a certain position, that I began to question the schooling. In those early days you were told to go here or there and you went. You were not told why. Nobody questioned it, you just went and it worked. You never had to think it out for yourself.' Today of course it would not be as easy because people want to know why a director is doing this or that.

'As a young man going into something that you knew nothing about at the time, were you impressed by the fact that it was repeatedly rammed down your throat that - we are the D'Oyly Carte, this is how Mr Gilbert and Mr Sullivan directed it one hundred years ago, and that's why we want to do it exactly the same?'

'Yes, I was impressed by that. Really impressed, and it made us work a lot harder to get things right. This is why today I am a stickler for words. Amateurs do an awful lot of things to words that are not as good as what was actually written. It might be just an occasional word here and there, but it alters the whole meaning.

When I joined, I thought, this was silly. I had been in rep. In rep you have to get the jist of the words across and more often than not make a lot of it up. But not with Gilbert. At rehearsals Mr Godfrey would say to me, 'what note are you singing there, what word is that?' and I said to him, 'Mr Godfrey you might as well know, you petrify me. I am terrified when I come to these rehearsals.' He said, 'Oh John, please don't be like that. It's only because I am interested in you that I want it put right.'

I literally went home and started from scratch again. It's no good learning Gilbert's libretto as if it were repertory libretto. You can't do that. This is word for word. I was taught the hard way myself – but they were right. It certainly pays off in the end.

'So you believe that D'Oyly Carte did try to maintain the tradition that Gilbert established through his own direction?'

'I certainly think that. Whatever the D'Oyly Carte was, or whatever they might be blamed for, they tendered and savoured those operas with great care and affection, and the reason the operas are as popular today as ever, is purely because of this care and attention. It was their work that did it. We know they are wonderful works, and their preservation has to be largely down to the Cartes.

'You were playing small parts or chorus for that first eight year period, and if Peter Pratt was ill you took over. Were you taking over fairly regularly?'

'Oh yes, I did quite a lot towards the end. I never wanted to, and he didn't want me to either because, I think, in many cases he objected to me. I think, but I don't know, that he was a bit disgruntled and discontented with the company. I believe he wrote an awful letter to the D'Oyly Carte at the time when he left, but that is none of my business. I remember it was in Oxford, when the meetings were on.

We had meetings every year and we had to go in and see Freddie Lloyd and arrange our next tour. I would never have more than one tour on my contract, and I never would have an option on it. An option to me was very one-sided. They can say they want you back, and you had to go. We had this meeting in Oxford at The Randolf Hotel, which was with Freddie Lloyd. I thought, why have I got to go to a hotel to have a meeting, why can't I be like everybody else and have it in the theatre; it was there he told me that Peter Pratt was leaving and that they wanted me to take over. I just said 'oh yes, very well.' It was kind of my duty. If I had a choice I would have said 'pick somebody else', but after I had been there for eight years, this is what you are there for, now the time has come to do that. I just said 'very well.' That's all I did say because it was a shock, it was really a shock for me I think.'

'How much do you believe you changed the characters, from being the understudy to Peter Pratt to being the star, John Reed.'

'Well, I can't really say, except that I always played them as I wanted them played. I never ever copied Peter. I never watched Peter from the wings or anything like that because I can't be a carbon copy of anybody,

I have to be me. I suppose having been in the company for so long the characters eventually took me over. I like to think I played Ko-Ko like a mischief, and that was the mischievous part of me. I remember when I played Jack Point, it was like the sentimental part of me, I mean, I can cry at will, I have a feeling for that; the parts that were difficult for me were the parts like the Major General, the high-voluted parts, whatever you wanted to call them. You couldn't find anyone further removed from the Major General or the First Sea Lord than me, and the Lord Chancellor. Those were the parts that I had to work on the most, and I think because of that work they actually became my better parts.

'Looking back, would you say you had a favourite part and a least favourite part.'

'I am asked that so many times and I don't really know. Perhaps it would be Ko-Ko – or Jack Point, I think. The second act as Jack Point, as a comedian or a funny man or character man, or whatever you want to call him gives you the opportunity to make people laugh, and you also want to know that you can move them to tears as well. I could see that I moved them to tears as the handkerchiefs came out. That was a reward to me. I used to have an old Director on BBC2 and he used to come and see the shows. If he wasn't crying when he came back to the dressing room after a Yeomen, I thought I wasn't very good tonight. As regards Ko-Ko, I think I brought a lot more dancing to it. I was a dancer. The dancing never bothered me. I would worry to death if I dropped a word or something like that, but if I fell on my bottom while I was dancing, it wouldn't bother me. The dancing was just easy to me, the music came easy to me as well.'

'How did you develop the characters, did you have any golden rules? Did you have to get your feet right?

'No, I don't think so. I must have worked on them a lot. I know when I became the character. I knew that when I put the costumes on, and the costumes began to fit me. For example eventually the Major General's costume was not a costume, it was my clothing I was putting on. It was mine, I could wear those costumes like I could wear my ordinary lounge suit. When they became my clothes , when the shoes and everything fitted right, that was when the character was me. I was a stickler for wanting everything right when I went on – my stockings had to be right. I had to spend a long time with my make-up and, I suppose, that was getting into the character. When I first played King Gama, I was sorry for him because the poor fellow had a hump on his back, an awful leg and everything else. No wonder he was twisted and one thing and another, so I was too nice to him. Somebody said that was a fault, so I thought, you want him nasty, good, I'll make him nasty; dirty the wig down and this lovely white wig, they greyed it and made it older; the make-up became bigger, then I really was a big King; they wanted more and I gave them more. I was brought up in business with my parents and the customer is always right, and they were the customers, as far as I was concerned. My whole ambition really was to please people out there, that's what I was there for. I used to think to myself, I may not have the best voice in the world, not be the best actor, and not the best singer, but you jolly well are going to hear me. I am here to tell a story and if I can't get this over to you, what's the good of my being up here.

Did you find that there were principals that you naturally were very comfortable with on stage?'

'Yes, having played all that time with the same people, I could be on stage and look into their eyes and know what kind of mood they were in and how to re-act. Don and Ken were always great to work with.

John with Donald Adams and Ken Sandford

'What about encores – did they allow you to go out of character and be as individual as you wished?'

To me any encore is out of character because no person comes back in the room again and says the same thing do they? You are now more yourself than you are the character, and you can have a bit of fun between you and the audience. That is the way that I thought and that's why I altered a lot of my encores.'

'Were you encouraged to do this by the D'Oyly Carte?'

'No, I wasn't really, not really encouraged. I don't know that anybody objected, they might have done, but what I used to do was do it first without saying anything and listen to the reaction. The first thing I did was in Ruddigore. That's the bang I introduced in the second act. I was standing waiting. Ken Sandford was on with Peggy Anne Jones and I was standing by all this scenery and stuff, and just before he says "But soft, someone comes," I pushed it all over, deliberately pushed it all over, and there was a crash, bang, wallop and there was a deathly hush for a minute, then the whole audience just erupted and Ken never moved, this is why they were so good. Ken never moved and said, 'but soft, someone comes'. The Stage Manager appeared and I said, 'I just happened to lean beside it and it all went flying'.

Kenneth Sandford,
Peggy Anne Jones and John

He got suspicious when I did it next time. It wasn't very long before Miss Carte wrote to me and asked me if I would cut it out as some of the fanatics didn't like it, so I said 'yes, yes, I would cut it out, you are the boss.' A week or so after that I got a letter back saying 'we would like you to put it back in again, we have had so many complaints with it being out'. What you try to do is please everybody but you can't!'

'So, did Miss Carte take an active interest in the shows?

If she did we wouldn't know about it. She certainly took an active interest in costumes. I remember, her coming to see a show – Yeomen – and everybody was on the stage. We all welcomed decent criticism, or to be told we were alright. Whenever Miss Carte would come in they used to say 'oh the Royal Family is in'. When she was in we welcomed her comments and criticisms. Tell us and we will try and put it right. All I got from this particular visit was that my shoes were scuffed, and I think Phoebe's pinafore dress was wrong in some way.

Isadore Godfrey hated me doing the twist which I occasionally put in before an encore. I felt it was popular with the young people. They were our future audience, but he hated it. They put the wings on me at the end of Iolanthe and I concocted this little string at the front. I would turn my back on the audience, pull the string and my wings used to flap. He hated that too. I wrote to Miss Carte and said, 'look, I don't want to upset anybody. Isadore doesn't like my flapping wings – what shall I do?" I got a letter back to say, ' it has to stay in, she likes it'; he went on hating it!

'What do you think was the funniest encore you ever did?'

'The funniest encore I ever did was jumping overboard in Pinafore. I had about five standard encores which included the semaphore flags which had been my idea. This particular night the fans called me back again, and when they start the music you have to go on. Well, I had nothing prepared, so I was moving off and doing all sorts of funny things, and thought, if this happens again, I will have something ready. So I decided to get a lifebelt. I told nobody. Sure enough the sixth encore was called. Nobody told me what to do, so I nipped my nose and jumped off the ship you see, and it was such a shock. The audience fell about laughing, the orchestra stopped playing because they wanted to know what had happened, they were standing up and looking over the top, it was absolute chaos; then I came back on with this lifebelt round my neck. The audience loved it and, of course, it was put in and taught to the understudy after that.

But, that night, I thought, what have I done this time? It's the devil that has got into you really. As an understudy, and working with whoever was taking the rehearsals and so forth, I always did as I was told because I knew that I had to fit in with other people. When it became my part and I was on my own and I put things in like this, in the majority of cases, nobody said anything, they belonged to me then. Of course, the encores I didn't change until later because I wanted them to be mine. I thought, you know I am doing all this that everybody else does. I am following Gilbert and Sullivan, but he didn't direct the encores, so if you want to make any sort of point at all, to become anything different from anybody else, then you have to make it your own particular part; that's why the audience loved the encores.'

'You must have played before many celebrities. I mean who can you remember particularly?'

with Prince Philip

'Well, of course, the Queen and other Royals came, and you know Charles came into my dressing room when he was very young. I think, apart from that, I think, we never really knew who would be in the audience really; when you are playing in London anybody could come to a matinée. I know that Donald Sinden always used to come round every first night to the dressing room. Danny La Rue the same. In America you never knew who might be in the audience. We met people from Little House on the Prairie, Jean Stapleton and many more.

'Why do you think that Bridget D'Oyly Carte, presumably, didn't allow them to film all the shows?'

'I don't know, but whatever it was, it was a great mistake. The only thing I can think of is that if anybody saw it on film or television, they might stop coming to see the live shows. I can't think of any other reason. I think it is the one big mistake that they did make. They should have had these on film the way they were done in those days. They should have been filmed because, now, there is only people like Ken and myself that know some of the business that goes on.

'Would you say you prefer Gilbert or Sullivan?'

'That's a difficult one, that really is a difficult one, I don't think I separate them, I don't think I can separate them, which I think is the proper way because they go so well together. I think in the past I would have said Gilbert because I am an actor and a singer, but I mean there is so much that needs the music to get both players and audience in the mood anyway.

'It's now more than twenty years since you hung up your boots for performing every night. 'Do you find yourself still going through the parts?

Yes - it's still there you know. It's like picking it out of some box or computer or something, it's just in there. When I am directing, which is a good thing for me, when I am directing I can prompt anybody without any prompt, without looking at the book pretty well. I never ever thought about playing any other part either. I always knew that I hadn't the heart to play Fairfax, for example. It's the same with acting in rep. I wasn't the leading man, I was the funny man, or the little character man, but I could have played it. I would have more feeling for those parts, more than any of the tenors that I have seen playing them, because I feel things as strongly, I am so sentimental. Comedy and tragedy must be so near together, they must be so near because I knew I could make people laugh. I knew it. I can get them to such a pitch in the encore that I can just wink at the audience and the whole thing fell apart, I do have that, I do have it. I knew that I had got it, let's say that I knew that I had got it, not that I have it. I am a shy person, I was always shy.

The times that I remember, I have stood in the
wings waiting to go on in a huge theatre in
America and thinking, what am I doing here?
God this is awful, all those people are going to
be looking at me, all those eyes looking at me,
then you get on and you work and it's alright.'

They were wonderful days, all fun and
enjoyment, but when you take over the big roles
it's different. Then you get a responsibility and
I was very conscientious. Even as an understudy,
I must say that every night before I went to sleep
I went through all the next night's opera. Just in
case Peter Pratt was off. I never wanted him off,
never. Mind you he never wanted me on either
I don't think.

I remember once he was ill in Manchester and he
didn't think he could finish the show. Mrs Blane,
rushed me into the costume and I thought at half
time I would pop in to see if he was alright.
I knocked at the door and went in, and he turned
his head away and said "I'm not going to look at
you, I'm not going to look at you, yes I'm alright,
I'll get through it, I'm alright, I'm alright."
He couldn't bear to see anybody else in the same
costume, I just didn't think of it like that at all. .

I was told to watch Peter from the wings.
I didn't like that, because I didn't want to be a
carbon copy of anybody. If I was going to make
any success whatsoever I wanted to be myself.
I think always your own personality must come
through somehow, and so I couldn't watch him
very well. I was embarrassed at watching him.
I never liked people watching me from the wings
either very much.

Six faces of the Peter Pratt years

The parts seemed to come so natural to me somehow. I'd always sung about the place and this was just another song I had to learn. I re-wrote those operas you know in the early days. When you've been in Rep, you get the main gist of the story and then the rest you fill in on your own. So I did the same with Gilbert and Sullivan. It all made sense. But I was wrong. I was picked up every other sentence by Isidore Godfrey saying "what's that word, what's that note?" and I thought "good heavens, this is different to what I thought it was really".

So I literally went home and started from scratch again learning every word and every note. Accuracy was drilled into me to such a degree that now I am a bit like that myself. If I go and watch a show and there's a wrong word crops up I hear it instantly and it disturbs me. Gilbert wrote so well, and each and every word is important. I suppose that's what it is, but it took me some time to recognise the importance.

It was rather an urgent project to get me ready for the parts. Peter Pratt, who had taken over when Martyn Green left the company, had run ahead of William Morgan, who had been understudy to Martyn. It had been considered that Morgan was growing too old to take over. How he felt about this I don't know. In any case he was still there and rather graciously started teaching me the business for the parts he had understudied for so long. At the same time "Snookie" Evans or Mrs. Darrell Fancourt, wife of the famous Darrell. I was the resident producer and I was tossed between her and Billy Morgan, with him telling me one thing at one rehearsal and her saying quite the reverse at the other. It was very difficult having to remember which instructions went with which teacher at whatever rehearsal. Finally I was forced to tell them how difficult it was – as kindly as I could – without making unnecessary troubles. From there on in it was Snookie alone who carried on with my training and I never worked again with Billy Morgan.

It was a great relief actually for I always had the feeling of jealousy towards me – natural I suppose, although it was totally unnecessary for at that time I had no idea that he had ever had designs on playing the parts himself.

There was a lot to do and less time than I imagined. After about a month or so Mr. Morgan left the company and I was the only cover. Dear old Don Adams was at a rehearsal with me and he was doing everything wrong, bless him. It was in the early days, and I was a bit of a pet of hers.

Then I made a mistake in the dialogue and she went 'tch', I can't stand 'tch.' Call me anything but 'tch'. There's no hope for anybody like that. And she did it again and I said 'I've only had one rehearsal on this you know Miss Evans.' 'Oh no you've had more..' I said 'excuse me I've only had one rehearsal on this.' 'Well, we'll just have to have more rehearsals' she said and started to follow me around but I wouldn't look at her. This went on for a while and although I was really hurt with Miss Evans it obviously had to stop.

For a large lady she always dressed nicely. She came in one day looking particularly attractive so I walked over and said 'erm, Snooky', which you were only allowed to do once or twice. 'Snooky, you look absolutely fabulous this morning, that hat is lovely.' 'Oh, do you like it darling' she said and immediately we were like that ever more. It's the only way to get on.

It was not very long – a few weeks – when it happened. In Leeds. I had very poor digs with no decent bathroom so I arrived early at the theatre, unshaven, meaning to wash and shower there. I was met at the door and told that I "was on" that evening and I had to rush to a rehearsal as the principles were there already waiting at a Church Hall a little way down the same street. After I realised it was no joke and that Peter Pratt was not well, I hurried to the hall and was rushed through Ruddigore.

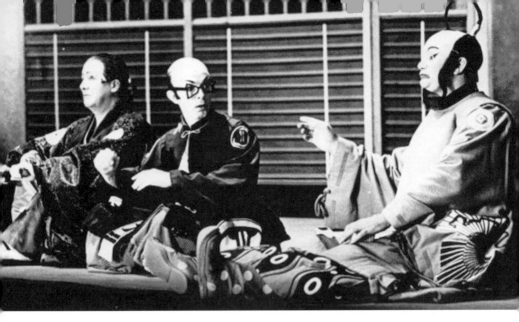

Seems like a dream – or perhaps a nightmare – but I had no time to dwell on it for when it was over I had to start worrying about the next night, which was KoKo in the Mikado.

This meant another galloped rehearsal and to my horror I discovered that all the props, fans etc were Peter's own and he kept them locked up, which meant I had to spend the afternoon buying the necessary materials to make the things I needed. So many of the trick fans I used were invented that very day, added and improved as my time with the company went on. The next eight years meant many such times, playing the roles for Peter, mainly as so called "trial" shows having had previous notification by letter that "in your capacity as understudy you are requested to play the part of......on such a date" with details of whether it was a matinee, evening or both.

It was a fantastic learning experience working with the likes of Leonard Osborne, Fisher Morgan and Darrell Fancourt. The first time I went on with Darrell I played the Major in Patience and I had to walk up stage with him and he whispered "John, I'm blind in this eye so watch out when you're at this side 'cause I can't see you." And Darrell had no stage whisper whatsoever. He had a big blustering voice. He was a wonderful man and I was at this side of the stage with him and he had to go across to Ella and say "Ella, what is the meaning of this" and he walked across and she said, "leave us" and he had to turn round and come back to me. As he walked back towards me he somehow got his costume caught. He couldn't see what had happened and ended up crawling back with his nose inches off the ground. And he looked at me and in his quietest voice said "I nearly went 'arse over tip there'". And the whole of the audience heard him and roared with laughter. But that was Darrell's stage whisper. He was a dear sweet man.

At the end of the 1959 tour plans were drawn up for the following year's programme. We were in Oxford performing and I was called for my interview with Mr. Lloyd. I wondered why it had to be at the Randolph Hotel and not in the office at the theatre. A week or so before my meeting I had been staying with Mary Sansom and her husband Allan Barrett in Wolverhampton with dear Cue. This was Mrs. Cuerton, a darling amusing landlady, who was also a strong Spiritualist. In the course of our stay, she had said that I would take over some very important parts and Mary also – but not the parts that Mary had been understudying. We were all highly amused at the forecast and laughed a lot about it knowing nothing of the situation developing within the company. As I prepared for my meeting at the Randolph I thought of Cue and her premonition.

Mary Sansom

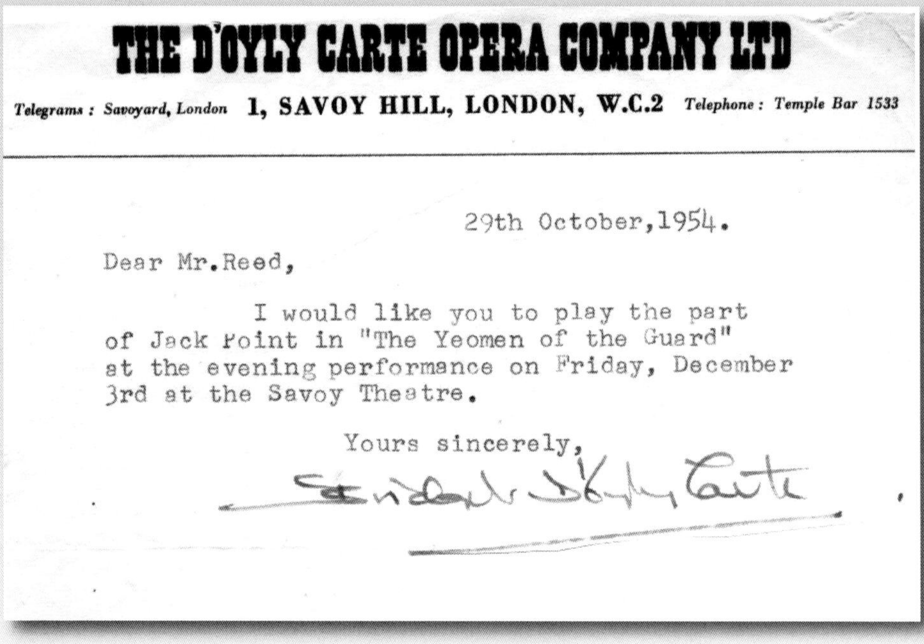

THE D'OYLY CARTE OPERA COMPANY LTD

Telegrams : *Savoyard, London*   **1, SAVOY HILL, LONDON, W.C.2**   Telephone : *Temple Bar 1533*

29th October, 1954.

Dear Mr. Reed,

        I would like you to play the part
of Jack Point in "The Yeomen of the Guard"
at the evening performance on Friday, December
3rd at the Savoy Theatre.

      Yours sincerely,

Quite simply and perfectly straightforward Mr. Lloyd said – "Mr. Pratt is leaving the company and we would like you to play the parts."

"All right Mr. Lloyd" I said almost as if it was my duty, but I recognised of course that the playing was now over and it was time to get serious. All the time that had been spent on me in preparing, the rehearsals, the costumes, the wigs, the fittings. Now it was time to "pay up." So the beginning of the next tour saw me as a principle and oh yes! Mary Sansom became a principle soprano just as dear Cue had predicted – again as Cue predicted she was not playing the parts she had been studying.

And so the road to becoming a D'Oyly Carte legend began.

His presence, it would seem was soon felt, which may account for Peter Pratt's relatively short reign after the long ones of his illustrious predecessors Martyn Green and Henry Lytton.

John Reed's 28 years with the D'Oyly Carte Opera Company turned out to be its golden era.

I like to think of it like that. I can tell you something else. Suddenly, people were acting. That inevitable semi-circle for which the D'OylyCarte was known, always with the girls in front and the boys behind, crumbled.

Everything became natural, more believable. We weren't regulated, not so stilted. We began to believe what we were saying and the performances became much more intense.

Breaking down conceptions wasn't always easy, though.

The things John had to put up with, even as the established star of the company, beggar belief. The more he talks about them, the more realisation dawns that management attitudes hadn't changed since Gilbert and Sullivan's time.

D'Oyly Carte performed 48 weeks a year which, in John's time as patter man, included seven tours to America and one each to Denmark, Rome and Australasia, as well as perpetual touring in the UK.

His weekly wage with D'Oyly Carte was £100 and £3 was what the understudy got if they went on.

It's amazing he stood for it for long.

Mr Lloyd announces John Reed's elevation to principal comedian

Some of John's more famous roles

Chapter 7

" I'LL NEVER TAKE WORK I'M UNABLE TO DO"

D'Oyly Carte Principal

For the next fourteen years or more I was totally, completely and utterly immersed in my roles with the D'Oyly Carte. This meant literally every performance – matinee and evening. When we went on tours to America I was expected to be involved with all the publicity interviews for both radio, television and newspapers. The demands were so heavy that I had little time to see the country we were visiting.

It seemed that the people playing the contralto roles – the Katishas, Fairy Queens etc. were also expected to perform in all the shows.
Other principles had their free nights. It was an exhausting itinerary and I attended few parties – reserving my energy for the performances.

I was coming to the opinion that "all work and no play makes Johnny a dull boy" and came to the conclusion that perhaps I should give up at least one part to enable me to see something of the sights and cities that we visited. I began discussions with the management emphasizing that it would also be an excellent opportunity for my understudy to gain experience and prepare him for the task when I retired. The discussions seemed to go on for ever, but eventually it was agreed that the Major General, which was the smallest and my least favourite part would be the one I would drop. This was one of the parts that has no "warming up". You enter at the deep end with the Major General's song which of course is your one and only chance to make any success of the role. If you fell then there is little chance to redeem yourself. If I were to stand back now and judge my performance I would have to say I thought it was one of my better parts, but the song caused me much anxiety. Although I sang it thousands of times on stage I went over it millions of times more in the wings, which is not a good thing to do, for by the time you get on stage and you are in the middle of singing, your brain can often say "I have sung this line before", frightening, but I could never ever refrain from this habit of going over my lines in the wings.

We were preparing for another American tour and I was looking forward to the trip and having the nights of "Pirates of Penzance" free to sightsee and party with one less responsibility.

I remember we were negotiating our performance fees with the General Manager, Fredrick Lloyd. He had been told that the American Management expected me to play all the roles including the Major General. Bang. That was the end of my free time. So I said "no"
– I would not tour under those conditions. The Americans insisted. So did I. Eventually Mr Lloyd persuaded me to join the tour and only play Pirates on Press nights.

I had been given to understand that if I did not go on tour I would be putting the company in jeopardy and there was every possibility that the whole tour would be called off. I went. Would you believe, the press nights were the only nights that "Pirates" was played. Well not quite…
… there were two shows in Los Angeles. I hired a car and got really excited about driving to Disneyland as it seemed everyone else had done just that. Came the morning of the big day, my phone rang and I was asked to stand by as Howard Williamson, who was to take over the part was not well and may not be able to play that night. As it happened he did – but I did not get to Disneyland, but spent the entire day standing by in the Theatre.

On our return to England, our first date was Manchester and the Monday opening was to be The Gondoliers. Tuesday it was "The Pirates of Penzance" and the part of the Major General was no longer mine. I had made sure of this after my experience in America. Since I had been away from home in London for so long I decided to return after the performance of "The Gondoliers" to have a day at home. Nicki and "Sheba" my boxer dog came with me to Manchester on the Monday morning. While making up for "The Gondoliers" that evening, Bert Newby the touring producer, came into my dressing room and instinctively I knew something was wrong as he only came to see me when asking a favour. He told me Howard was unable to play the following night and would I do it – but Bert it is no longer my part I said and reminded him what had happened on the American tour.

"I know John" he said "but the understudy is not prepared and we do not want him on. All I can do is ask you." Of course there was nothing I could do but promise that I would play and I drove Nicki and Sheba back to London that night and returned to Manchester the following morning.

At the end of the week the then Touring Manager, Stanley Knight, came to see me at the theatre to tell me that since the part was no longer mine, I would have to be recompensed for performing in "Pirates" on the Tuesday evening. He advised me that I could either be paid for playing the part or have a night off in lieu.

He suggested I took a night off – as the payment would only be three pounds. I can hardly believe it happened this way – but by golly it did and that is the true story of my relinquishing the part of "Major General Stanley".

One does not change when one becomes a principle within a company – but I do believe that attitudes towards you change. I was determined not to let this happen and so the number one dressing room, instead of being like the "inner sanctum", became more like Grand Central Station. I had no desire to be alone in that room. I was so accustomed to being in the chorus room, where there was always so much fun and life.

Of course I saw many changes during my time with the D'Oyly Carte. When I had first joined I rarely took my car and indeed very few members had cars. So it was always the train call on moving day (usually Sunday) and as was said "only fish and actors travel on Sundays."

Train calls were arranged with separate compartments. The managers were in one; the principals in another; the staff, wardrobe mistress, assistants, stage carpenter etc. and then of course the chorus.

Cynthia Morey, who was playing the soprano roles – YumYum, Phyllis and Patience about this time, and I had become good friends, as indeed we are to this day, and usually spent our free time together. When it came to train calls we certainly had no desire to travel in separate compartments. Slowly the rules were relaxed and all this unnecessary segregation stopped. I believe before I joined the company, that men were expected to travel separately from the ladies – even married couples, travelling together was frowned upon.

Cynthia Morey as Phyllis

Once in Edinburgh it rained for the whole three weeks and Cynthia and I painted canvas after canvas for the whole time we were there. When we came to move on we managed a whole compartment in the train to ourselves and took the opportunity of holding an art exhibition with absolutely ridiculous prices on each oil painting, needless to say we sold none but we had a great time. Cynthia was always the life and soul of the party – full of ideas and I like to think that we sparked each other off with ideas for special birthday cards, which we made and painted for members of the cast.

Being a large company such birthdays were always cropping up.

I remember the night we were bombed. It was a Saturday evening in March. My dressing room was half below the street level with half of the window in fact looking directly onto the pavement. I remember it was frosted glass with bars for security reasons. The show was just over and we were all back in our dressing rooms hurrying to remove make-up and dressing in time to catch the pubs before they closed at eleven o'clock. Laughter and singing was all around when there was a huge explosion and I am sure everyone immediately realised it was an IRA bomb. I had got as far as my underclothes when it happened and I was standing close to the window. The glass was blown over me as the window smashed and I was literally blown off my feet to the wall opposite. Sheba seemed to land along side me and was also in a state of shock. It seemed almost immediately the voices of the Police were heard shouting something about another bomb expected to go off and that no one should leave by the stage door, but use the front of house entrance. After dressing very quickly I hurried out with a mystified Sheba on her lead very conscious of all the glass and mirrors, which one finds in theatre dressing rooms. The thought suddenly struck me that my brand new car had been parked on the opposite side of the road to the stage door. I remember grumbling, that no matter how early I arrived for a show I never seemed lucky enough to be able to park my car on the prime spot outside the stage door. You can be sure that this night I was grateful to discover that the blast had missed my car, but damaged all those that were in the prime areas.

Once outside, no one was allowed to go up the street anywhere near their vehicles and a taxi was the only way for me to get back to my digs with Sheba. This was a great disappointment. Being Saturday night, the usual practice was a dash home, no matter how far, but without a car it was impossible. Around 3 a.m. I rang the Police and was given permission to go and pick up my car. It was too late to drive home, but I was anxious to know the state of the car. I found it untouched – but no longer in the same parked position that I had left it. In fact it was way down the road, still locked up and to this day I puzzle how it got there and exactly how it was moved without the keys.

All the dressing room windows in the Opera House were on the same side of the building, and each one had been broken. Miraculously no one in the cast suffered a single scratch. Ken Sandford, who always dressed so quickly (I never managed to beat him) had already exited by

the stage door and was practically blown under one of the cars, but
thank heavens, emerged quite unscathed. I was given to understand
that the bomb was not meant for the theatre but for all the Law Courts
that surrounded us. On the following Monday we returned to the
theatre in the evening to find that the glass in the window frames was
back. When I got to my dressing room I found a rather large piece of
glass, shaped like a dagger, on my dressing room table, stuck into my
make-up removing cream. How easily it might have been.....
it doesn't bear thinking about. The Opera House in Manchester
still remains one of my favourite theatres.

It was easy to understand that once you were in the D'Oyly Carte
Opera Company, for me and many others, it became our "family"
and life. There was little time for anything else. Most Sundays were
spent travelling from one city to another and settling in to what ever
accommodation one had been fortunate (or unfortunate) to find.
Then first thing on Monday morning I usually headed for the theatre to
find the dressing rooms allotted. When you were in the chorus of
course, the earlier you arrived in the theatre the better place you could
find. As a principal the rooms had your name on the door. In some
cases theatres with less dressing room space meant having to share.
I usually shared with Ken Sandford, which always worked well.
We got on splendidly and it always suited me and I hoped it so for him.

There seemed to be rehearsals practically every day except when we
had a matinee. These rehearsals would be for an understudy going on
because of illness, or where an understudy was being given a run for
the first time and needed to work with the regular performers.
There were also the special nights with extra special visitors such as
Her Majesty the Queen, Prince Charles, Mr. Churchill, Field Marshall
Montgomery.

I remember one evening at the Princess Theatre (now the Shaftesbury)
that Winston and Mrs Churchill sat in the front row of the stalls, very
clearly seen from the stage. He was pointing out people in the
company and you could almost hear the rasping voice asking his wife
"who's that one?"

A room had been prepared for him to have his whiskey during the interval and there he was, seated glass of whiskey already in hand when Bruce Worsley, the touring manager at that time, said to him "soda Sir?"

Winston nodded and Bruce reached for the syphon and poised it over Winston's glass. Someone nearby asked a question and Churchill turned quickly to answer as Bruce squirted the soda syphon – missed the glass and saturated the ex- Prime Minister's legs. Behind the curtain we waited to go up on the second act. Having had the applause for Isadore Godfrey, conducting that evening, we could not understand the extra delay and could hear the audience getting restless and voices from the "gods" (upper circle) crying "come on Winnie." We all discovered later of course that "Winnie" was being dried off. Eventually he made his appearance to a tremendous cheer, and when at his seat in the stalls he turned slowly and gave the whole audience the victory V sign. Later I was to learn the whiskey episode was not the only amusing incident attached to the Churchill story that evening.

Harry Haste was at that time our stage carpenter responsible for the "get in and get out" at the theatres. This included the scenery, the skips, props everything that moves. He had responsibility of moving all this equipment from city to city, both in this country and overseas, whether by boat, train or plane.

He was a large man – both up and out – slow moving and with a dry sense of humour and a voice like gravel. He used to tell me a joke every time we met, and when I repeat them I somehow must finish the punch line in my impersonation of his gravelly voice, which makes it twice as funny but still not as amusing as when delivered by the man himself.

He knew of Winston's expected attendance to the opera that night and went to a great deal of trouble to acquire a Rolls Royce. The manager of the company at that time, Bruce Worsley, and his assistant Michael Freshwater were waiting for Churchill's arrival at the front of the theatre, with great anticipation. They were dressed up and keyed up. Eventually a Rolls glided to a halt in front of them. Instantly they walked towards the car door. There in the back seat of the limousine, quite clearly was the silhouette of Churchill, slumped with cigar and black homburg. They bowed very low and together, as no doubt rehearsed, saying "good evening Sir". From the interior came that unmistakable gravel voice "what the bloody hell do you want" – that was the Harry we all knew. No type of expense spared for a good laugh.

Meetings with the Royal Family were always special. I was in the Princess Theatre and I think it's called the Shaftesbury now. I was in the dressing room very near the stage, and people used to pop in to see me, especially my stage mum. You know about my mum, my stage mum? It all started the first time I went on as KoKo. Betti Lloyd-Jones came up to me and said - you looked so sweet I wanted to Mother you. So I said "be my mother" and for 17 years or more, every night she would come in to my dressing room, kiss me and wish me "good luck son."

My theatrical 'mum'

And it got like a routine and even when she had a car accident and was unable to perform I got a letter saying "good luck son." That's how close this company were. Anyhow I was in that dressing room and Betty had been in and she said, "Prince Charles is in tonight," I thought "hahaha", she said "yes he is, and I'll tell you where he is sitting." She must have looked through the curtains and saw him in the front row. So when I went on, I went along the front row and sure enough I stopped, I could see this silhouette, and I could see these ears sticking out. So, my eyesight was good then, it must have been, and then after the show, I didn't think anything more about it, and I was scrubbing my face or something and getting the make-up off, and there was a knock at the door and I shouted "come in", thinking that it was somebody from the company, and in walked Prince Charles, Commander Somebody or other and Miss Peebles. They were there. What do you say to a little boy? I asked if he had enjoyed the show – and he said yes – except Katisha was horrible. I said "she isn't horrible at all really, she's a very pretty girl," so I sent for Gillian, and she joined us.

Later on we were at another Theatre and he came again, and we had to meet the Queen between the first act and the second act. Then you had to leave to get ready for the next act. And as I was walking out, Charles was standing in front of me. "Let me see," he said, "it's six years since I last saw you." He was charming. He loved Gilbert and Sullivan. Whenever the Queen came of course, you usually knew. They would tell you beforehand, but occasionally she arrived without us being told. You could tell. There was usually a row of men all sitting behind. Her bodyguards I suppose. Safety.

On another occasion we had to go to Windsor Castle to perform Pinafore. Everybody is vetted and we were in what they call the Knight's Room

Windsor Castle

I think or something similar. And there were pictures all around of the Queen. Huge great paintings, and the next room where we were to perform was a ballroom, and they had built a new set for the occasion. Now, when I did encores or anything I had to go out of this door and run along the corridor beside all this lovely furniture and armour, and come in the other door. Well we did the performance and you could see them all sitting there, watching. The whole group, Princess Margaret and everybody. We did it well. It was all over and then there was this reception afterwards and we had to go and meet the Queen and the Queen Mum. We kept our costumes on and I went to the Queen first and then along to the Queen Mum. "Oh' she said "you've got nothing to drink or eat, you must have something" so she called this lackey and gave me the glass of wine and something to eat. I loved her from that moment, she was just like a mum.

Anyhow then we came out and we had to get dressed and go into this reception. By the time we got in the gannets had been before us and finished all the food. Freddy Lloyd came up. He put his arm round me and said it had been a huge success and asked "is everything alright?" And I said "no everything isn't all right Freddy. I've been in there and we've done our duty and now we find there's not a thing to eat, and there's not anywhere to put my bottom to eat it". "Oh' he said, "well there's some strawberries coming in just now you must have some of those".

Afterwards they apparently discovered that about half a canteen of cutlery vanished from the reception. There was a big uproar in the company. A note went round that all the items had to be returned. I can remember going in the wings shortly afterwards and I could see something glitter on the top of a basket, and I looked and there was a knife, spoon and fork . They were put down in front of the office. All the missing items were returned. But I just thought - in America they expect you to take things. That's why they put names on ashtrays. It's advertising really. Not from the Palace.

Chapter 8

"MY FRIENDS,
I APPEAL
TO YOU"

The Fans

It seems that the whole of the company used to be very intrigued by my fans. I am sure that all my predecessors had theirs as well.

Shortly after I took over the principle role these fans began to appear and would often follow me home, mainly to discover where I lived. I would try my utmost to dodge them by driving quickly up a side street but for all my attempts they ultimately discovered I was living in a quiet little mews, and when I would go out to my car in the morning I would find a note stuck in the windscreen wiper of the car. Perhaps it was a kind of game, and by my trying to run away I was making it worse.

I remember one morning going out of the house to find this well known fan of the company just standing looking up at the home. 10 o'clock in the morning. I simply could not understand it.

I have always wanted to do my job to the best of my ability but then to finish and go back to my home and private life. To me it was the only way to be true. To play KoKo or Jack Point or any other part in the theatre, but to stop acting after the show was over and come out of the door as John Reed. In fact I'm not capable of acting off stage at all. It really is quite beyond me. Maybe I disappointed my fans in this way, I don't know. But just as I was most sincere about what ever part I was playing so I was as sincere about myself and my private life.

When I first started one of my fans was a bus conductress.
She subsequently became a bus driver. She would sit in the theatre in
full uniform and wait at the stage door afterwards. Always so faithful.
One time I bought myself a new car – a white MG. I loved that little car.
She used to drive a van and often would follow the company around the
country, from Bournemouth to Liverpool to Manchester or wherever.
She painted her car white also and not content with that painted around
it all my characters. Very flattering but most embarrassing to me to have
this van following me from wherever I was playing back to London
after the show on Saturday night. I always tried to drive home for the
weekend. I remember playing in Hull and after two Mikado's I rushed
to my car to race home for the weekend. I maneuvered the winding road
and finally found the A1, which would lead me back to London.
Picking up speed, I suddenly saw it. The van, moving very slowly and
waiting for me. The A1 was the only road I could possibly take and she
knew it. I was to say the least irritated and on this occasion she spurted
past me rather than following me as was the usual pattern.

A few miles further on I drove into thick fog. I hate driving in fog,
especially when I am tired – and I was tired that night. The fog slowed
me down. My fan in the van waved me down and walked back to my
car and said " John you must be very tired, may I lead you back to
London?"

This she did and how grateful I was for the sight of the van that night.
Twice she pulled off the A1, asking me if I would like coffee.
She opened the van door and it contained everything but the kitchen
sink and pretty soon I had my coffee. The second time she stopped
I had closed my eyes and maybe I nodded off for a minute or so.
I wakened up to find her and her friend walking quietly round the
car to see if I was awake and to allow me a few minutes respite.

Where does one get this kind of devotion? At that moment I realised the
value of fans and changed my whole attitude. How lucky I was to have
such fans, and how much I needed them. I always wanted friends,
needed them, searched for them. It didn't matter what package they

Signing autographs

came in. I made up my mind there and then I was not about to turn
them away. I loved them all from then on. Thank you little bus driver
– you taught me such a lesson. For those years and years of devotion
and love, let me say how much I appreciate it, perhaps it was just plain
embarrassment in the beginning and I shied away from it and didn't
realise, especially in the Gilbert and Sullivan way of life that so much
of this sort of thing goes with the job.

Chapter 9

"TO CHARM AND PLEASE ITS DEVOTEES WE'VE DONE OUR LITTLE BEST"

Theatrical digs

Most of these digs have now disappeared, but many members of the company have such wonderful stories to tell. Prior to joining the D'Oyly Carte I had been in several so called "Boarding Houses" but I must confess that until I started touring I had no idea that they could be so good, so awful, such fun, so cold and threadbare.

Once we had been on tour in America and on return York was one of the cities we would visit. The procedure for accommodation was that the company would write in advance to the places we were to visit and newspapers would publish the necessary advertisement asking for people who were interested in accommodating us to notify them.

Pre curtain up the company would announce that "the digs letters were in from Manchester, Hanley, Edinburgh or wherever." There was then an absolutely mad rush from the dressing room to the prompt corner with much pushing and shoving and hands in the air waving the letters shouting – one here for two girls, or "two doubles and no animals". There was lots of laughter at the same time and in the end I may say a few rude remarks. Cynthia Morey seemed to be extremely good at choosing just the right letter and invariably did very well. Of course at that time we were on very low wages and certainly had to keep expenses down. I started at £9 a week and after one year was given a £2 rise because I was a principal understudy. Amazing isn't it? Out of that I also had to run my car although we did get a small travel allowance if we didn't go on the train. However getting back to digs, and Cynthia. She certainly was a good picker. One particular choice of hers was full board including four meals a day (breakfast in bed) for 35 shillings a week. That achievement could never have been beaten I'm sure.

In Belfast at Mrs. Mac's, the higher you went in the house the cheaper it got. Cynthia and Alice Hynd, another dear friend, usually beat me to the attic and I ended up in a bedroom on the first floor, which was probably 5 shillings a week more – but I did have a wardrobe, whereas the girls had to do with a large old empty grandfather clock, devoid of its innards. The digs letters were a constant source of amusement.

"Me beds' good springs" and . . .

"I'm used to theatre people – my mother was in the wardrobe for two years"

"Have no dogs hoping to hear from you."

They may sound funny, but some of the landladies were the salt of the earth and would put themselves out to see you satisfied.

Going back to Mrs. Mac in Belfast. She was extremely kind. She liked her little drink though each evening and would cross the road to her favourite pub and return by taxi. It was hilarious to see her stagger into the cab at one side of the road and tumble out on the other. Cynthia, Alice, Johnny Fryatt and myself would always try to get into digs together, it just trebled the amusement. Some were a little stricter and television (when it arrived) was switched off at a certain time whether you were interested or not. Some digs also had their "lights out" embargo. Even today when any of us get together no matter how long since we last met the noise and laughter is tremendous and the reminiscences are invariably about times in those digs.

In Leeds I had a sort of bedsit on the first floor with a dear old lady who carried my meals upstairs. She remarked one day as she puffed upstairs carrying the tray of food into my room – "oh Mr. Reed I'm so tired I could just fall prostitute on that bed." Most of these stories happened it seems during our chorus days and being a principal you missed so much.

The funniest story was not mine but one of Jack Habbick's, a very jovial Scot. He was in a boarding house in Edinburgh with three or four other choristers. They had bought themselves a large bottle of Sherry for a "wee dram" after the show. The following day, Jack, examining the sherry said, "hey, this sherry has gone down – she must be drinking our sherry."

This didn't suit them at all and the next night after it had gone down still further they decided on a scheme to get their own back. They decided to "spend a penny" in the bottle and if it went down further to repeat the gesture. It did – so they did. At the end of the week when it was almost empty, the landlady said "I hope you don't mind I saw you had a bottle of sherry so I have been putting some in your soup every day!"

Theatrical digs. They certainly were the good old days, before hotels – or rather before we could afford hotels. I remember Julia Goss telling me a story of her experience in digs in Leeds. As I remember the digs were very satisfactory, the landlady charming and the house itself extremely clean. Breakfast was from half past eight to nine in the morning. After 2 or 3 days, the landlady asked Julia if everything was satisfactory for her. "Everything is fine" replied Julia. "Just one little thing" she added. "Breakfast is a little early for me. You see we work very late and I do like a lie in in the morning."

The landlady replied eagerly – "that is no problem my dear you can have breakfast at whatever time you wish." Everything was solved thought Julia and the next morning came downstairs to breakfast at around 11 o'clock. "Did you have a good nights sleep?" said the landlady. "Perfectly" said Julia "It was so wonderful to be able to sleep on a little longer".

"Wonderful" said the landlady. "I have your breakfast all ready for you. I have been keeping it warm." This of course was exactly what the land lady had done. She cooked the egg at the same time as usual and it was all prepared on a tray. The dear soul was so eager to please, what on earth could poor Julia say except "thank you" and carry on with her two hour and four minute egg.

Chapter 10

WHAT A TALE
OF COCK
AND BULL!

Jack and the heel

I suppose my days in the chorus were the happiest time I had in the company. The people one joins with always remain rather special, and although they have all gone their separate ways, many into other theatrical companies or even other jobs of work, if ever we do meet there is always the same bond.

I have always likened the company to a large family and indeed there is no denying the fact that it was. Many many years ago whilst in the chorus, I happened to be sitting next to Jack Habbick, a baritone from the Glasgow area, who became a good friend. Jack always wore rubber heels on his shoes. They were round I remember with one screw in the centre to hold the heel in place and you could always turn it round on the heel as it wore down. One day he lost one of the heels and went to buy a replacement. They came in pairs. Since he needed only one to fasten to the shoe we began to play with the other at each interval in the dressing room. I remember spinning the thing round and asking it questions and we printed "yes" on one side and "no" on the other. All very silly really but it became quite a standing joke. At the end of the week as we were packing to move on to the next theatre on the tour, Jack handed the heel to me and said "you can have it John."

"Have it Jack – I never want to see the thing again as long as I live" I would reply. I never actually figured out just how he did it but at the next theatre, although I was in a different dressing room and nowhere near Jack, when I opened my locked up make-up case there was the heel in the middle on my make-up towel.

I never mentioned this to Jack, or he to me but that heel passed between Jack and I for years and years without either of us ever referring to it again. Sometimes it was weeks before it turned up again – sometimes a month or even six months. The methods of passing it were quite hilarious at times – often quite hilarious. On many occasions they were delivered on stage – never of course by me for indeed everyone in the company were in on the joke.

At one time I had a Policeman come to the stage door and ask for Mr Habbick. Jack rushed to the door wondering no doubt what he had done and the Policeman handed over the heel saying "I believe this belongs to you."

I was in Harrogate in some digs and he was on the floor up above and I was wakened up at 3 o clock in the morning with this tap tap tapping. I went to the window and there was the heel dangling beside it - and he was upstairs asleep.

Oh it's been sent backwards and forwards and one thing and another.

The best thing we ever did I think I got Johnny Fryatt's mother to bake it into a mince pie. A little round mince pie and prior to that, for weeks we had turned the conversation round to mince pies and how you should never refuse one and never break one because that was unlucky.

Anyhow these cakes came. John got the one that he wanted and he offered Jack a mince pie! We had really impressed on him - never refuse one. That's refusing good luck. So he knew he had to take it. So he took the mince pie. He was all primed for this sort of business and I was outside the door and I heard this going off and then suddenly I heard a shout as he sunk his teeth into the special pie – *it's the bloody heel*!

He had a bath once and I just threw the heel over and it landed in the bath water in front of him. We never spoke of it.

One year he said to me "Happy New Year" John and he left the heel in my hand and I just walked away and never said anything. We never ever mentioned it. Everybody in the Company knew about the heel. It was a regular thing.

Well Jack and I fell out. It was awful. They made him stage manager and the job was too much for Jack. Somebody had come off stage and left his costume on the floor and thrown his wig down somewhere, and Jack had to go and tell him to pick his costume up and put the wig on the block. It was just too much for Jack and at the same time for some reason we quarrelled. And I regret it to this day and so did he. Anyhow years passed by. I'd left the Company and Nicki and I had a fire at the bottom of the garden. Nicki shouted –' John can you come up here' and he handed me this elastoplast tin.. It was all charred and I opened it and inside was the heel. I said "Oh my God it's the heel Nicki. I must send this to Jack, This will put things right between us."

Jack died that very same day. That heel was burning at the same time as him practically. Incredible.

We buried the heel in the garden of the house we lived in in London. We had a wall with flowers and I put it right down there covered with flowers. That was the end. That heel had been passed around for fifteen years at least.

On Tour

Home in London;
The hotels in Bournemouth;
and American visitors admire
the view over Halifax, West Yorkshire

Meeting Her Majesty The Queen and (below) The Prime Minister

*At home in Halifax with St. Thomas's Church in the background.
It is here that John's ashes will be buried*

Gilvan

Tom Round and John
admire the painting
of Isadore Godfrey

John with
Peggy Anne Jones

Barbeque time! On tour

John with Pat Leonard

*Two favourite roles -
Sir Joseph, and Ko-Ko
with his platinum disk,
OBE and citation*

Elizabeth the Second

105

Master class
with Valerie Masterson

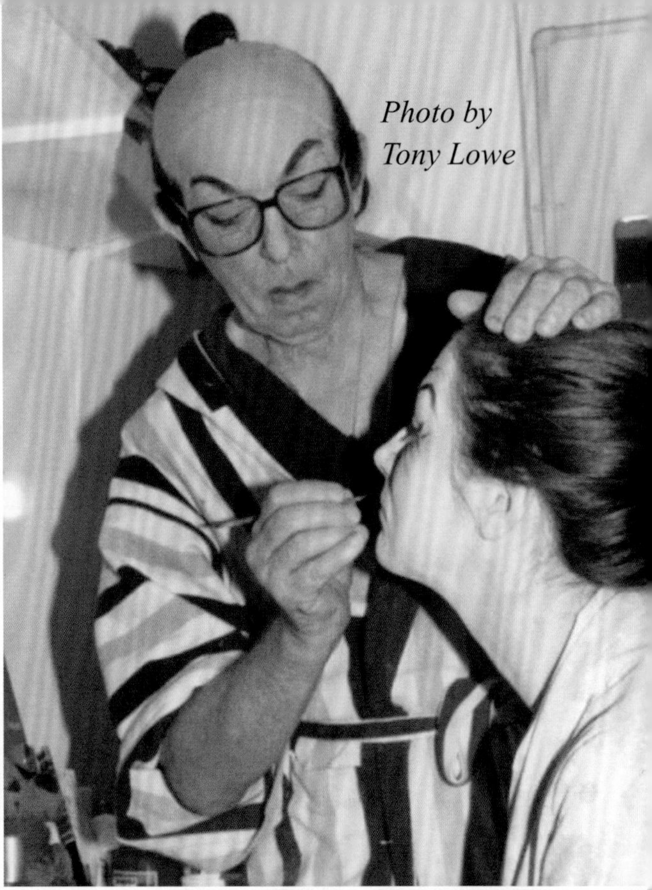

Photo by
Tony Lowe

FIRE EXIT

104

Directing around the world

Buxton

BBC's Songs
Of Praise

David Turner
admires his figurine

Derby -
Champions

In Brussels - photo by Tony Lowe

With friends

Julia, Ken, John, Gillian, Don, Tom - In concert in Buxton

His last "Together Again"

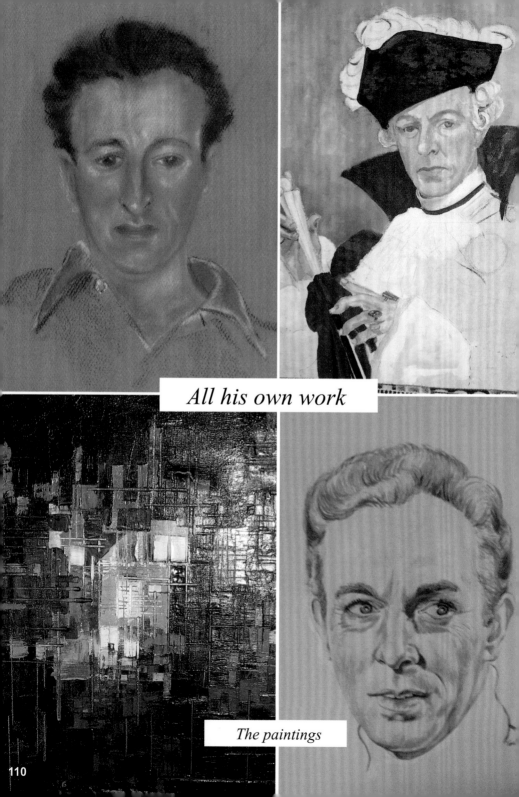

All his own work

The paintings

The Figurines

Chapter 11

"UNFRIENDED, UNPROTECTED AND ALONE"

The D'Oyly Carte Family. That is who we were. The artists, both principals and chorus, in those days always travelled together on train calls, stayed in those wonderful theatrical digs together, rehearsed and performed all the time together, when it was possible did concerts for hospitals in the afternoon, and in the evening were entertained and sang at various musicians' clubs, always together.

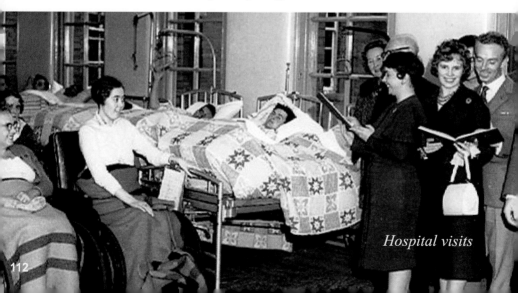

Hospital visits

There was a time when about 16 of us decided to travel around by caravan trailers. By this time most of us were moving around in our own cars. Naturally we all had to be on the same caravan site, winter and summer alike. I hated my caravans, dragging that huge trailer behind my car, but I wasn't going to miss the fun.

John with some of his caravan pals

They were wonderful, happy days and but for the D'Oyly Carte may never have been, including the visits to the United States. The excitement that went around when we heard rumours of our visits there was a thrill I shall never forget. My first visit to America was in 1955-56. It lasted nine months, as I recall. One can see quite a lot of a country in that time, sightseeing and being entertained the way the Company was.

That first trip to America was the one that always holds the best memories for me. We went all over, from east to west, New York, Boston, Chicago, across the vast country to Los Angeles, San Francisco, Denver, wonderful Central City, Colorado, and so many more wonderful places, all exciting and new. On that first visit I was principal understudy, doing small parts and chorus, and so had much less responsibility. For all visits thereafter , of course, I was playing the principal comic roles and a lot of time was taken up with publicity for the Company and the shows.

Most of our time was spent travelling around Britain. There were of course trips to Ireland and trips to play in Rome and Denmark. It seems now, looking back, that there was always something happening, such as the visits of the Queen to the shows, the Queen Mother's visit in

Aberdeen, when the theatre was decorated with thousands of beautiful yellow roses, and Prince Charles' memorable visit to see Mikado, when he was just a small boy.

There was always a season in London at the end of all the touring around. I think I can say that everyone in the Company liked that, for it meant that we were in one place for at least 16 weeks. By this time I had my home in London, as had many others and we travelled back each weekend no matter where we were in England, just to have a little time at home. Those 16 weeks or so were so very good to us.

Those so-called Last Nights were very special. In the program there would be a question mark for the first act, two question marks for the second act, and, of course, three for the third. The audience knew practically as much as we did, for not until we got into the theatre did we know what we were to do. In those days, the orchestra would play a mixed-up overture, jumping from one opera to another; we would do, perhaps, the second act of Mikado and not know what was to happen until we returned to our dressing rooms after that. Then it might be the first act of Princess Ida or whatever costume the wardrobe department had laid out for us when we were busy on the stage. This tradition grew as the years went on and got wilder and crazier, with each principal not letting another principal know what he or she was to do, so as to attempt to confuse them on stage.

The beginning of this craziness was, as I remember, Trial by Jury. I was at that time an understudy which meant that I also played small parts - the Judge in Trial was one of them. On the Last Night, we were to do that opera perfectly straight, but everyone was to be in the wrong costume. For instance the bride was to be Yum Yum from the Mikado, the defendant Ralph Rackstraw from Pinafore. I was to wear the Chancellor's robes from Iolanthe, the jurymen in the box were pirates, the girls of the chorus were dressed in the dresses from Patience, and other principals who were not in that particular opera were on this occasion in the courtroom as the Pirate King, the Duke and Duchess of Plazo-Toro, Mad Margaret, Patience herself, and the Police Sergeant from Pirates, played by Kenneth Sandford at that time. It was a blaze of colour and fun.

It was to be played straight (what a laugh); just everything was happening. There were streamers, balloons, the Policeman taking chocolates around to the pirates, Patience giving out bottles of milk, Mad Meg jumping up at the oddest moments, shouting ''Basingstoke,'' and all the time the opera was being sung straight (no one could deny that). This was all before my entrance; I thought, ''if I go on now no one will even notice,'' so I asked a stagehand standing by if he had a bicycle. He had, or got one quickly from somewhere, and I made my entrance in the robes and wig of the Lord Chancellor of England on a bike.

This was the start of many such wonderful last nights to which our marvellous fans would almost go crazy to see; and indeed the demand for seats for those last nights, was so great that they had to apply, and there was a ballot to pick out the lucky ones who made it.

Flower Power rules!
John Reed
with Christene Palmer

Miss Carte didn't approve of the last nights, but the audience loved them. I always said they should have had a matinée as well because many people couldn't get in to see the shows and they booked so early and so quickly. I think the first one I did was John Wellington Wells. I knew I had a teapot and was doing something with it. Then I played three Patience's. I did one as a sort of hippy flower person with Christene Palmer. I did another as an Australian with the corks on my hat and for the last one I thought I would do a Travolta but Ken Sandford beat me to it so I thought I'd go as a Rocker – in leather! A special wig was created and dressed in leather and chains I bared my chest and right across my chest was tattooed 'Barclays'. Barclays Bank were big supporters at the time.

My Last Tour

My last tour with the company was to Australia, I remember I was not too keen to go so far from England, especially as it was such a long flight, and I have never liked flying anyway. Not that I am alone. It really is amazing the number of people who are in the same boat, or should that be plane? Eventually I was persuaded by Mr. Lloyd, who was the manager of the company. It was indeed a long and rather dreary flight. About 25 hours flying time, touching down at Bombay, and I think, Brunei. Actually I took the two stops as an opportunity to sleep, as I most certainly cannot do so when in the air.

We landed safely in Sydney and the whole company, with the exception of Derek Glynne, the impresario, who was responsible for the company's tour of Australia, and myself, left almost immediately for Canberra, yet another flight. No joy, no rapture!

Canberra was to be our first date in Australia, the first ever, as the company had never toured in this vast country before. As I recall, we landed in Sydney about 9am. The company left soon after this, but come 6pm, I was still in the VIP lounge.

I slept for a little while on what seemed a sumptuous settee. I had been told very little as to what was to happen, or if I had been told, I was far too tired to take it in and much too weary to indeed care, I was waiting for Derek, who was busy seeing people.

Business of course, he worked so hard on that tour, and also lost a great deal of money for his trouble on that project. Derek and his wife Kate I liked very much, and indeed still do, though I see very little of them these days. They are both out of the country a great deal, mainly tours of Australia with other theatrical adventures. So still in the VIP lounge, Derek came back and told me we were to fly to Melbourne to do publicity, including an appearance on the Dan Laine Show.

Television was very big in Australia and now, I am sure, is bigger than ever. Anyhow, when I finally got to the studio in Melbourne my costume for Sir Joseph Porter was already hanging there. So it was first make-up, then on with the costume, and I went on and did the television show hardly aware of what I was doing, suffering from jet lag, and not having slept well for what seemed like days.

Years later, imagine my horror when I got a letter from Don Laine Enterprises to say that the show had been sold for viewing in America, and that particular show was to be screened. Now I know this to be true as I received cheques for the showings. What they must be like I shudder to think. Being in such a state of exhaustion, they would hardly be top viewing, but as long as I do not have to see them. I know of many artists, like myself, who cannot bear to see themselves on the screen.

When I read in the programme of what I was to do here – The Legend of Gilbert and Sullivan – I stopped, and thought. I realised that it really was a legend. But having been part of it, so to speak, for 30 years, it never occurred to me to be so, until I returned to the company for the last few weeks, at the final break up, the final performance at the Adelphi. The end of the D'Oyly Carte, family of G&S, the end of an era.

I was involved 28 years playing with the company, and even when I left the D'Oyly Carte, I was in some other company or concert or production, still playing G&S - the legend.

I never thought about the actual men, but more about D'Oyly Carte. Here I had a connection with one actual member of the family, Dame Bridget, with whom I was a friend, and who came to my home.

I had always maintained that one need not necessarily know of the author, playmate, or whatever to act, play, or sing the characters he, or in this case, they had written about. It was not necessary to know of Shakespeare's association with Anne Hathaway to play a good King Lear, Shylock or Ophelia. Neither, I thought, was it necessary to know of Gilbert and Sullivan's lives to play King Gama, Pooh Bah, or Mad Margaret. But having spent much time in Stratford-upon-Avon when playing with the D'Oyly Carte at the Memorial Theatre, passing Shakespeare's house of his birth each day, soaking up the atmosphere of Stratford must, I realise, now help, just as I had soaked up the atmosphere of G&S when with the company all those years.

But with me, it was so gradual, and being so busy with the operas themselves I never troubled myself with dates of meetings or dates of the operas, or of the so-called quarrels, until much later. In fact, I have come to learn much more since I left the company than during the period that I was with them. At the beginning, I of course, saw much more of the operas as complete pieces, than when actually performing. For lengthy periods I was in my dressing room, changing costumes, or make-up, or even just resting until my next entrance. But when producing or directing I was able to once again appreciate the operas as a whole.

I decided to leave the company. I wished to do other things. After all, I had been in the D'Oyly Carte for 28 years; and if I wished to direct or play something other than Gilbert and Sullivan, it was time before I got too old or even lost the desire to do those other things.

This decision was very good to me, because of the other things I have done. In all those years the company may have played eight times in the United States while I was with them; since I left I have been to work in America at least 15 times. True, it was mainly to either play or direct the operas; but also I got away from them and acted in other operas, for example, Offenbach with the Washington Opera.

Chapter 12

"IN SAILING O'ER LIFE'S OCEAN WIDE NO DOUBT THE HEART SHOULD BE YOUR GUIDE"

You left the D'Oyly Carte in 1979?

I threw myself out of work and it wasn't until I had made the move that I asked myself – what are you going to do? Who knows you? I was just one part of a company. We were all together. There was no "principalitis" or anything like that. I waited at the end of a queue like everyone else.

To my relief I did not have to wait long – and I was grateful to the D'Oyly Carte for giving me another break. Somebody rang them and asked if they could recommend someone to go and direct. It was Boulder University, in Colorado. They had an opera school and were going to start doing G&S. The D'Oyly Carte told them I was leaving the company and would be free. They wrote to me and invited me to go and direct – and off I went on the next stage of my life to Boulder.

Now this was very strange. I had never been in America alone before. I'd had the Company, my "family" around me. There I was standing in the middle of Denver airport wondering who I was going to meet and how they would know me. I am surrounded with all my luggage and these two Professors came up to me and said "you're John Reed aren't you" and I said - "yes, how on earth did you know" and they said "we recognised you by your clothes!" The English clothes. Otherwise I'd have been standing there yet!

My challenge was to direct two Gilbert and Sullivan operas - Mikado and Iolanthe - in two months. Here I was in beautiful Boulder surrounded by the Rockies. It was not quite what I thought it would be. I was working with students from twenty years old who had mastered in music, singing, and indeed, all the different sections of theatre.

What actually happens is Professor Jackson, whose whole idea the experiment was, sends out to other universities all over America notices of the coming Gilbert and Sullivan season naming the operas and classes, etc; those interested then fly down or send tapes, if it really is too far to audition for the leading roles, so I may get a leading lady from Montreal, (indeed I did), Chicago, Texas or any place, even local, such as Colorado Springs.

I always arrived a week before starting to rehearse – to get adjusted to the altitude as Boulder is a mile or more above sea level. Then all those wonderful people started to arrive. Little did I think I would return year after year. It became almost like going home.

That was my first introduction to America without my "family." It was the start of a new and exciting "career." For someone who did not like flying I began to do more and more – two, three or four times a year across the "pond." I went to Washington to the Kennedy Centre to do Trial by Jury. That was wonderful what a set they built for me . A real solid set. The Judge could actually slide down the banister rail – I had a ball and afterwards they said "John since it's such a small part will you play a small part in this other opera 'Monsieur Choufleuri' by Offenbach and I said "yes, sure!" I hadn't learned anything new for so long. Could I still do it. It was in French. I've never learned anything in French. How Valerie and Gillian managed with all their Operatic work I'll never know – miraculous. Well, I learned the part and I was told that everyone understood my French better than anyone else! Mine was schoolboy French. Mine was "la plume de ma tante" – really basic.

I returned to Boulder for thirteen annual productions and Nicki and I were made honorary citizens. Wonderful place. Wonderful memories. And that's how my new career began.

And you then directed and performed all over the States?

Washington I suppose was the first real start. Just as you found me in Harrogate and I came to direct the Savoyards, a similar thing happened there. Two representatives of the New York Gilbert & Sullivan Players turned up to ask if I would go and play with them in New York. That was another adventure. I went and did lots of things in New York. I had a very good time.

The Dick Cavett show was one of the hottest TV shows of the time and I remember getting this phone call first thing one morning asking if I would go on the show. I said yes and he said - "I'd like to do a duet with you." I said OK what would you like to sing. He said I would like to sing the Nightmare Song! I said - as a duet? He said "yes" and I said OK. You know how it goes - 'when you're lying awake with a dismal headache'......He took it slow and I took it fast, slow and fast all the way through – and it worked and we had fun. I don't know whether anybody's heard of Dick Cavett. He was very famous in those days. It's a long time ago.

Then I saw you playing Ko-Ko in Los Angeles

Yes I remember. I was directing. It was in the theatre where they have the awards and it was very strange because that Theatre was opened by the D'Oyly Carte so downstairs in the dressing rooms is the plaque – Opened by The D'Oyly Carte.

The previous year I had been singing as a guest artist in Trial by Jury and HMS Pinafore. The concerts were so successful that they asked me to return to sing Ko-Ko.

Originally they were planned to be purely concert versions, but I cannot stand still. I expect the singers to move. So they asked if I would produce some movement and we added props and everyone seemed to enjoy it, especially the performers. It was so short a visit I have difficulty in remembering their names. I mean, to fly anyone from England to do a matinée and an evening performance sounds quite the craziest thing ever. I of course did lots of interviews for publicity, which is really no hardship at all - in fact, most pleasant, doing a broadcast live from the restaurant at the Music Centre while you are having a meal of whatever you desire from the menu. Well I chat away in that most pleasant atmosphere and never think for one moment that thousands of people are listening to me.

The two concert shows in Los Angeles were a great success. The Americans are most hospitable, kind, and I suppose, having been there so often, I find them very similar to the English.

Where else did you direct or perform in America?

Boulder, New York with NYGAS, professional companies in Daytona Beach and also the big Cleveland Opera Company. I went to Dallas; Tulsa, Oklahoma; Salt Lake City; Louisville, Kentucky; Daytona Beach; Albequerque, New Mexico; and Washington DC. I've never been out of work, never.

I return to England to do two concerts or so before going back to the D'Oyly Carte at the Adelphi Theatre in London where I shall be playing for the close of the company – strange having left the company over two years ago in Perth, Australia playing Sir Joseph Porter – I shall now play the part again as the company ends.

Alone in his Savoy dressing room

The most awful thing I ever did was the one man show " I have a Song to Sing Oh!" For two weeks I was alone in my old dressing room at the Savoy. Two weeks in the Savoy alone in the Theatre that I'd played so many times with all my friends around me and it was awful to sit in that dressing room and hear "Mr Reed your call please." And that was the only call that went all night, nobody else. Nobody coming into my dressing room to say good luck love or whatever. I was lonely. I don't like one man shows at all.

When you returned from Australia was the Guest House in Bournemouth already in place?

No it wasn't. Nick was working at the Savoy and he was dissatisfied with the management and I said you don't have to stop there - for heaven's sake leave. So he left as well. And he bought this hotel down in Bournemouth and went to look after it and was very happy there whilst I went on Tour. There was one year when I only got home for two weeks out of 52 – and that was to change my clothes! I had always been away touring somewhere.

And you were there for quite a number of years.

Yes we were in Bournemouth for many years. Of course in the meantime I'd been up here. We met and you and the Savoyards were the reason for our moving to live in Halifax. It was such a happy time. I was tired of London and tired of Bournemouth. It's a lovely place but the only time I got home was holiday time. You couldn't park your car anywhere and if you went to the supermarket you just couldn't get near.

Have you enjoyed directing amateurs? What kind of pleasure has it given you?

It has given me a lot of pleasure. They are still exactly the same as we are. They are there because they want to be there. They're there because they love it and I want to pass on anything that I can to them. I've had such a good time myself I want to give some of that good time back - it's as simple as that.

When you came to direct The Savoyards you stayed at my house and that's when you started a new hobby – machine knitting.

I was in Leeds at the Grand just opposite Lewis's it was and I went in. I saw this woman doing this knitting. I stood there for a while and said I'll have one of those and they loaded it in the car there and then. I never read a book, never looked at it. Put it together myself and then I started. And it was wonderful. Within a couple of days I could knit a pullover. Couldn't get back from the theatre quick enough to start knitting. It did lace as well. It was all computerised. I was having trouble with the lace so I went back to the lady at Lewis's and said what's the matter with this I can't get it to work. She showed me and suggested that I practiced while she went down to the storeroom. So I sat at this machine and when I looked up I had an audience around me. I told my "audience" how wonderful they were! She immediately sold three machines when she returned.

I'd go to the office in the morning and come home at night and there were scarves all over the floor! Metres of scarves. You could nearly mummify yourself.

It was great fun. I was the first one I think to get you to wash up at home. I used to cook for him because I wasn't doing anything in those days and I think once I got him to cook for me. When I left I was hiding all these little post-it notes – get washing up, get washing up. I hid them in layers of plates and all over the house. Did you ever find them?

Yes I did. Cooking was another of John's skills. I can tell you if John Reed has cooked for you once you'd like him to cook for you forever. Forever.

I must tell you about the latest thing I have got. I can't read now, I can see fine but I can't read. I have trouble with the computer, when I work on it I have my nose about an inch off the glass but weighing anything with these digital scales was very difficult. I have a little magnifying glass that I always carry with me and I go to it but its hard work.

So you started with The Savoyards and we went to America..

What I remember about that was you playing KoKo. And he would always do the curtain speech as he does in Buxton and I would wait in the dressing room to make him up and he perspired like mad and I couldn't keep the grease paint on his face.

Then you went to the Isle of Man and did a few shows there.

Yes I did. I would have done more but that's when I was ill. That was fun I liked that.

And then you came out of retirement with the Nomads. And you've enjoyed three Nomad productions specially for Buxton.

Yes – I love them they're lovely, they really are lovely.
We really have a good time.

Is there anything you still want to achieve?

I don't think so. The one thing that I wanted to do was to create a part myself. Not to follow in the footsteps of Henry Lytton or Martyn Green, I wanted to be the first one to play a role. I suppose in a way that this one man show did that in a way. The other thing was that I played The Sorcerer with the D'Oyly Carte. That hadn't been played for a long time. I think the costumes were destroyed during the war or something and they brought it out again and they wanted me to play it as a Cockney and that hadn't been done before so I felt I was creating a kind of "new" role.

John Wellington Wells

What about funny moments on stage?

Oh, I talked to Val about this one the other day. It's my funniest moment I think. It was the Ducal party entering in The Gondoliers. I was there with Gillian and Valerie sitting opposite. We were pulled across the back of the stage and the gondola got stuck. Beside me there was a picnic basket with all sorts of bottles of wine, and wine glasses and cups, saucers and sandwiches or something and they were on my lap. As the boat bumped everything fell into my lap. I am ready to stand up and get on to the stage and sing Sunny Spanish shore.But before I could move I had to pick everything that had fallen. I think I put a cup on each finger, and I had something under my arm, and everyone had something as they moved out of the gondola. I don't know what Valerie got in the end but she might have had the sandwiches, and we got on the stage and I started "From the sunny Spanish shore."

Then it was Gillian's turn and then Valerie and it finished up with Luiz who I think was Philip Potter. By that time he couldn't control himself and all he sang was "pu, pu, pu, pu, pu, pu, pu."He could not get a word out.

The awful thing about it was there was nowhere to put any of the picnic items so we had to go through the whole scene carrying everything. We just couldn't look at one another at all. And then we walked off and Gill and I fell in the wings killing ourselves but the awful part was that poor Valerie and Philip Potter were left to carry on with their love scene still carrying the picnic utensils. Oh that was the funniest moment ever. My goodness!

The most embarrassing thing I think was in America. We had a new floor cloth and I was playing Gama. When I started as Gama I was sorry for him - who wouldn't be. There was quite a lot he had to go through, and I was sorry for the poor man. They thought he was a bit too nice. I said 'do you want him nasty?' I said 'well alright will you get a red wig down for me.' Then I started on my make-up and I thought of him as being sort of paralysed down this side poor man.

So I got this mortician's wax which I used to make a false nose. It always had a wart and it even had little hairs coming out of the wart. Not for the audience – they wouldn't see it, but for the chorus. I asked Pauline Reece 'how many of these have we got Miss Reece?' She couldn't remember but said she would go upstairs to count them. She used to come and pick the wart off at the end and look after them for me.

Well this particular evening I had this big false nose on and I was really nasty and I found

King Gama

how easy it was. I could pin point my eyes and really look at them, and almost spit at them. I would have to say I enjoyed the new character. Well I was delivering the words - "the girl has beauty, virtue, wit, charity and pluck," and as I said "pluck," my nose dropped off. It was a new one and I thought "Oh my God I'll step on it - and it's wax." So I spent the rest of the speech - "would it be kind to parade these qualities before your eyes" searching for it - and I got it! I got it on the end of my walking stick which I then carried over my shoulder until my exit. That was a memory. Well it's funny now when I think about it, but it was very embarrassing then.

Then there was the scene with the Duchess in The Gondoliers. A waiter came onstage holding an ashtray whilst I smoked this cigar and the Duchess sang " On the day that I was wed." I never liked to distract – but what can you do when you have a cigar in your mouth and smoke is going up and you're walking across to the waiter to put the ash in the ashtray? And a scene developed. I looked at the waiter. And the cigar and the smoke. Finally I would stand on his foot.

Duke and the cigar

He didn't move. So I did it again a bit harder and he still didn't move. So next time I would grind it into the ground. He still didn't move and I just used to walk off – and then he walked off – with a limp!!!

So I said to him one day – wouldn't it be marvellous if I could blow smoke in one ear and it would come out of the other? He just looked at me and I said – ' it can be done! If you get some piping and put it up under your wig with a little thing behind your ear and another one at the other side, I could blow through here and it would come out the other side.' I was really joking. When it came to the next matinee the waiter came up and said 'I've got it in.' ' You've got what in?' 'The pipe!' I couldn't refuse to do it . So I went over, took a mouthful of smoke and blew it in – and out it came at the other side – and it stopped the show!

Although its 22/23 years since you left the Company you have kept in very close touch with your old friends.

Somebody rang me up that I hadn't heard from in a long time and said "Hello John. I bet you can't guess who this is." I said no. Well just try was the caller's response. And I said is it Philip Potter and she said no its Christene Palmer! She has such a deep voice you know. Now she rings up and says Hello John this is Philip. Very funny that. Lot's of people ring up.

'Cowboy' John in Central City

One of the big joys you always talked about was being with the D'Oyly Carte on tours and in particular your visits to Central City

Oh yes – what happy memories of Central City. It's near Boulder. I think the D'Oyly Carte were the first company that went there. Central City, was a wonderful place. I slept in the same bed that Mae West had slept in. Not many people can say that! She had a special sort of bridge built from her house, so she could walk across to the theatre, not touching the street.

Bruce Worsley our General Manager at the time bought a gold mine when he was there. The gold was there but it was the expense of getting the stuff out I think. If I had bought a gold mine I would have been down there picking it myself. It was a gold mining area and they said it used to be the richest square mile in America. Since it did mining a lot of Welsh people went over there. Welsh singers and so forth and that's how the Opera House came to be built. And we had a wonderful time. Denver is a mile above sea level and Central City is higher still. I can't breathe up there it's terrible. They still remember the D'Oyly Carte.

Now it's like Las Vegas. It's all gambling now and not a bit like it used to be but some of the same people are there. When we went the Sheriff and people used to come to meet us and we used to drink with them in little bars afterwards. I used to say to the Sheriff - we don't have guns in England. We don't carry guns like that and he used to say - it's never been fired John, it's never been fired. I was always pulling his leg about it. We would visit Central City for a couple of weeks and the night before we left nobody went to bed. Nobody, they were all up. And you were with the friends you made in that time. They were lifelong friends. I still contact them. We had to leave very early in the morning and there were buses to take us down to Denver. There were tears and people brought coffee and flowers and everything else as we left and it was heartbreaking. We got so fond of the place. As we were pulling away I was in the back of the car and there was the Sheriff standing in the middle of the road with his arms above his head waving. Goodbye - and he took his gun out and fired two shots in the air. Those sort of things were lovely memories.

So if you look at all the touring you did with the D'Oyly Carte which did you enjoy the most? Was it America, Australia, Denmark. Didn't you go to Denmark?

Yes we went to Denmark. Tremendous fun. But I can say that I was just as happy touring round England. Yes America was nice but do you know I always used to shed a tear or two because I never wanted to leave home. I'm a real home bird. What I'm doing touring around heaven only knows.

Flying isn't one of your favourite pastimes.

No it isn't. The first time we went to America it was to be on the Queen Mary. I bought an enormous cabin trunk that opened with drawers in and everything and all the clothes I was going to wear. There was a strike and all the crew were going to walk off the Queen Mary. Queen Mary was a rude word for a long time because all I got for the whole time I was on board was half a cup of cold coffee. There was nothing for breakfast in the morning. We were all on deck waiting for it to sail out and it didn't. We all went back to the Savoy and there was a big meeting and they said we were going to be flown across in a Stratocruiser.
I'd never been up in an aeroplane in my life and didn't particularly want

to. Incidentally I'd had to get rid of the trunk. I got it to the hotel and got things repacked in a small case.

Dear old Alan Styler was alive then. A funny man. I happened to be sitting beside him and I said "oh I don't like this very much. I don't think I'll like flying."

Alan Styler

'Oh there's nothing to worry about John' he said. 'Fasten your safety belt and repeat after me......'. "Our Father which art in Heaven" and to this day every time I get on the plane I say "Our Father which art in Heaven!"

I don't know how I did all that flying. You have no idea what a worrier I am, I'm terrible. I just sat and smoked. I smoked an awful lot. You know you could smoke in planes then.
You can't now I suppose.
It was worth it in the end, because I flew an awful lot to America and had some really wonderful times.

My funniest flying story was once when we hit an air pocket and the plane I am told dropped 600 feet. I thought the pilot said six, that was enough, but 600 feet! I think our stage manager blacked out, and there were screams and one thing and another and Abby Hadfield was in the 'loo' and she was sucked into the loo and the air hostess literally had to come and pull her out. She wanted me to tell the story at the Buxton Together Again concert but I said "Oh Darling I can't tell that there".

Alan was very mischievous. He would tell you something funny just as you were going to step on the stage. Then as you got on stage you saw the funny side of the joke and your first line would come out with a giggle.

Donald Adams came up to see me shortly before he died. I hadn't seen him for a long time and we laughed and joked about things that had happened. He and I did a promotional broadcast for the Company somewhere in America and also on the programme was an American who said that he was in touch with people from outer space.
I'm looking at this man because I'd been talking to him before we went on. He seemed an ordinary character. And suddenly all this came out. The world was a big ball and there was a hole in the top and there was another world inside of that. And I'm looking at that. And he said is there anything you want to ask. And I didn't say anything but Don said – You know about this hole in the top. Is there a theatre there and do you think the D'Oyly Carte will ever play there. The biggest plug we had on the tour.

Anyhow, Don spent an hour with us and we hugged him goodbye and we waved him away and I think a week after that he died.

How well known were the operas in countries where English was not the mother tongue?

We played in Rome. They audience knew the opera and a lot of people speak English anyway. It was the English speaking people that attended and I remember afterwards it was very exciting. "Bravo John Reed, Bravo John Reed" they chanted and they all walked forward and I thought I was going to be attacked.

On another occasion we played in Copenhagen. Wonderful, Wonderful Copenhagen. Flowers came up for the ladies. This was never allowed in the D'Oyly Carte. Then this biggest bunch of roses came up for me. Red roses .... and I'm stuck with them. I'd never been given a bouquet on the stage before and all the chorus were laughing like mad and they nearly fell about when the theatre manager came up and kissed me on both cheeks. That finished them all.

What is wonderful about America? There's such a lot of love in the parts that I visited – and particularly among the theatre community. The youngsters are great if you are directing or playing with them. They rush to give you a big hug. It's so friendly. At first I thought nobody would know me. I was wrong. I was walking down a street in Chicago and this man walked up to me and said "you're Mr Reed aren't you. John Reed?" And I said yes and I thought what on earth – in the street. And he said my wife's a fan of yours would you sign me this. He was a Solicitor or something and he opened his case and took a piece of paper out. I was gobsmacked.

I'll tell you another funny story from America. A lot of my time was spent doing publicity for the Company beforehand and I went to Hollywood and they asked me to do a one-hour radio programme. I went from Los Angeles by taxi and when I went into the studio there was this young woman doing a serious programme on classical music. She said she would introduce me after the record she was playing. And she did. "Now we're going from Bach and Beethoven into the world of Gilbert & Sullivan and I have with me a gentlemen who has been attached to the D'Oyly Carte Opera Company for many years and was actually given an OBE by the Queen of England. Would you please welcome Sir John Reed." I was so embarrassed. This was a live broadcast. So I let her go on with all her questions "what do you think about this Sir John, or "that Sir John"and I was right in the middle and I couldn't do anything. After an hour I thought - I can't tell her now poor darling. Could she see me out? I said yes certainly. And she'd brought me things from her garden. What a sweet person. And we got back to my taxi and she said "thank you Sir John it's been wonderful meeting you and I do hope we meet again" and she held her hand out and she dropped into a curtsy. I literally fell into the taxi. I was giggling and the taxi driver thought I was mental.

*All his own work...
the models*

Let's turn our attention to your hobbies – and in particular your model figurines

I have a delft rack that goes round the lounge and I collected the Capo di Monte figurines but as I looked at them I could see that the costumes for KoKo and the Pirate King were wrong. And I kept looking at them and I thought 'I could do better myself.' and so I started. I used to model a lot and once I started I couldn't stop. I modelled all my characters and I think I must have made, with all those I've given away about 60. Nicki used to paint them. It's air drying clay, so you have to be quick to model it. The last one I started was of you playing the cymbals with your leg up like this, when you were in Sorcerer.

I thought the costumes of mine were more correct than the others. They're not fired or anything like that, but they are dried and painted and varnished and they look damned good I hasten to say. So I have the whole set. As a matter of fact the people that did your Mikado figurine came up and photographed mine because they look rather like the people that played the parts. I knew them so well, so little touches of costumes I could get right because I had seen them so often, and just carried them in my memory. I've got a Pooh Bah there that I think has got to be perfect. The colours and everything.

And what about your painting.

Now that's the biggest blow of all, I have trouble with my eyes. I wasn't reading very well and so I said I must have some more glasses. I'd been reading in bed and fell asleep on my glasses, so we went down to get a new pair and the optician discovered that there was something the matter with my eye and they were going to have to phone the Doctor.

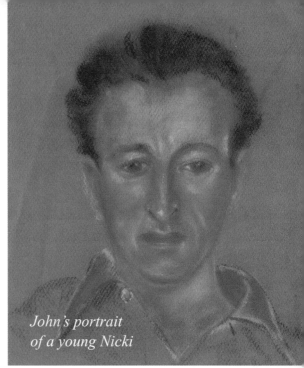

John's portrait of a young Nicki

The shock was so great that when I came out I think I was completely blind. It was the sun but I had to inch my way round the shops to get back, Nicki had gone to put some money in the meter, and I didn't dare cross the road because of the traffic and I waited until people had gathered round and I went with them towards the car park. I got in the car and I broke my heart completely. Now I had driven my car down there that morning to get these glasses but I couldn't drive back and I've never driven since.

I can't drive anymore, because the on-coming traffic is so close before I see it. I'm still driving of course but I'm sitting in the passenger seat and I'm there going round every corner more tired than when I used to drive before. So no more painting and the modelling, that's gone. I had this knitting machine left in the attic, so Nick came to my room and said 'John, you'll have to get rid of that.' It was all covered over and I said 'Nicki, I can't get rid of it, I can't let it go, I've had so many other things taken away from me I can't just give that up as well.'

Later I lay in bed and I thought I'll make it work again. So I got it out and I put it up in the spare room. It's got hundreds of needles and of course I'm not seeing very well ..... but I got it knitting again. It was like learning from scratch. I'd forgotten everything and to make matters worse I can't read the books to see what goes on. So I am having to bring it from somewhere in my mind. It was just that I didn't want to give everything up. I'm so determined when I go like that. It's awful growing older, it really is. I put things down now and I say "where have I put my glasses." I've got to that stage now.

You still cook?

Oh yes. Age Concern came to the door. This lady wanted to know if I really was John Reed. I said 'well yes I'm John Reed.' That's how it started. They offered me all these aids. I had my talking watch, which gives me the time and then I discovered a 'talking' weighing machine for weighing your flour and sugar and everything else. So I'm well away now. I used to have to bend right down to see what the scales said. Now I just stand back and chuck the stuff in. The new scales say 4 ounces or zero ounces and all this sort of thing. It talks to me so I'm well away, I have no difficulty there. No difficulty cooking any more. Except I also have a new microwave, which is a combination thing. That doesn't talk. It's got the grill, the microwave itself and an ordinary convection oven and one day, not seeing too well I pressed the wrong button. I burnt some jam tarts and set fire to the thing, these big flames were coming out of it. So now I have a big magnifying glass beside it to see that I am not going to burn anything else . There was a lot of smoke in my house, I nearly had the fire-engine there.

You also have these wonderful novelty security devices?

Yes (Laughing) Oh well I have a dog that barks if you come near the house. You don't have to walk it, you don't have to feed it. It's a box and the dog barks if anyone approaches the house. Then I have another device - one in the front and one at the back - if you touch the window in the sunroom at the back the light will go on and the music will start, and there's one in the kitchen a bad area too, but there are lights all round the house and if anybody comes to the front door we can see them on television, from a little television camera.

John, you came with me to Buxton in '93, and we made a little promotional film of Buxton. Would you have guessed then that this Festival would still be here today and attract the people it does?.

I remember thinking what a marvellous idea. I must say I've never seen so many happy faces as there are in Buxton during the Festival. Everybody looks pleasant and they all enjoy themselves, and I think it's a wonderful thing. I really do Ian.

I think that if you go back to the original D'Oyly Carte days you always had

It's fun, it's friendly - it's for all the family. Happy scene's at the Buxton G&S Festival

this very happy atmosphere in the theatre, which was quite unique.

You came a stranger but you left feeling part of the family. Here in Buxton it's that same feeling. It's wonderful. You know when the D'Oyly Carte got together it was, and I'm not exaggerating one little bit, it was a real family. I mean we travelled all the time together; we were there when people got married; people had their children. I remember Alan Styler having a daughter, and as the Lieutenant he had a line in Yeomen of the Guard which read, 'I have daughters.' And the day his daughter was born he stood on the stage, and he looked at me and I had just heard about his new daughter, Bridget he called her, after Bridget, and twitched one side of his face and said "I have daughters,". which sent me clean off. They couldn't send me up very often, but that did it I think.

We talk about happiness on stage. It really was happiness with us when we went on. For instance, I used to say to Gillian, "come on you old bag, let's get on here" and she used to say "alright you gas bag". I was called a gas bag because I talked so much. So we started this bag family. I think they used to come up and ask "can I be in the bag family?" Mrs Blayne the wardrobe Mistress was the Laundry Bag, Anne Sessions, in those days wore a lot of jewellery and she was the jewel bag, and there was a girl, I'm not going to mention any names, we called her the overnight bag. Jon Ellison? I'm sure he won't mind me telling you this, for his own reasons was called the tool bag. You'll have to think that one out. And so they used to conduct this, I was the gas bag, we were like a mother and father were Gillian and I. So that's what the atmosphere was in the company wherever we went.

What about the films you made - the Mikado and Pinafore?

They were bad films. I'm sorry about that. They used cheap film or something. I think they are pretty awful. We filmed in the, Golders Green Theatre

The black bow

Tell me about your meeting with Lord Elwyn Jones?

I was playing the Chancellor at Sadlers Wells theatre when I met Lord Elwyn Jones who was then the Chancellor of England himself. I was presented to him after the performance and found him an extremely intelligent and pleasant person. He remarked on the cloak I was wearing and how it appeared to be in a better condition than his own – except there was one thing missing – a flat bow which should sit on the back of the neck.

The following day I had a wonderful surprise. It was a small parcel containing a photograph of himself – and the black bow of which we had spoken. The accompanying note read: "Thank you for a most scintillating performance." I never did attach it to my costume though I had it framed and placed in a prominent position at home. I met him again at a performance of "Trial by Jury" which was performed in Middle Temple. The Queen Mother was there – she did love the Operas. I was last to go on and it had been arranged, though it was intended to be a surprise that I would sing a duet with the Lord Chancellor. We sang the first solo in Iolanthe – The Law is the True Embodiment. It was quite a riot and the audience would not stop applauding. As I led him off-stage he asked if we should do it again! And we did! A really wonderful evening.

What was your reaction John, when you got the letter through the mailbox saying that they would like to bestow the OBE?

Oh! I was frightened. They said not to tell anybody. Well you know me I'm a blabbermouth, and I had to keep this to myself. Everybody had seen the letter, because people used to gather round to read my fan mail. I said 'Oh! It is just another fan letter' or something like this - but they knew darned well it wasn't that.

I didn't know what to expect but it wasn't difficult. It wasn't as bad as going on stage for the first time, I'll tell you that. I went with my two sisters. They were very excited.

At the Investiture with his two sisters

It must be impossible for the Queen to know what needs to be known about everyone she is investing. Bless her dear heart. I went up to her and she said to me "Why are you receiving this"? And I thought well if you don't know darling! Because all the time in the music gallery they were playing Tit Willow and all my songs. All my songs were being played up there. What I called my songs in those days and so I said 'well Gilbert and Sullivan'. 'Oh yes' she said, because she used to come regularly. How can she possibly know everyone that she has to meet.

Miss Carte was there also, she was with Freddy Lloyd I think. She was a sweet person, a very nice person. She asked me to go see her. She wanted me to have a new hat for Bunthorne. She was shy, very shy, very lovely, and she took me for a meal at the Savoy. I wrote and thanked her and said "I would like to return the compliment sometime - would you come and have a meal with Nick and I and I added: 'p.s. I make smashing chocolate eclaires.' She wrote back saying she would love to come and added her own 'p.s. incidentally I love chocolate éclairs!'

John with Dame Bridget D'Oyly Carte

So Miss Carte used to visit us. She would take off her shoes and get on the settee and have a scotch. We did it quite often. She was a wonderful, wonderful shy person. I never knew they protected her like they did – just like the Queen I suppose. And I didn't know she had died. There is a picture of me somewhere, Bridget and I, and there's this parcel passing between us. People thought that she was giving me something. It wasn't that at all, I had come back from America and I'd brought her a gift. I didn't know until she had died. I hadn't the chance to write or visit. We were kept very much apart from the family. She never once came round to the dressing room. She was a really nice person.

John, centre, with Freddy Lloyd and Harold Wilson

142

Happy D'Oyly Carte days

More D'Oyly Carte moments

Henry Halls son Michael,
Nicki and Donald Synden
- at home in London

*Cynthia Morey, Muriel Harding, Jeffrey Skitch, Jennifer Toye
and John party on Jumbo Shrimps in Pasadena*

Not more spaghetti!

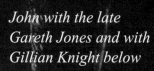

*John with the late
Gareth Jones and with
Gillian Knight below*

Chapter 13

OH TO BE
WAFTED AWAY,
FROM THIS
BLACK ACELDAMA
OF SORROW

I hear the soft note

A few months before the D'Oyly Carte Opera Company closed, I received
a request from them to return to play my old parts with them in Iolanthe,
Pinafore, and John Wellington Wells in the Sorcerer. I was actually in
America when I received the letter. The company was at this time in a
very bad way, I gathered, financially, for there was lots of publicity as to
whether or not they would survive. I said I would return immediately.
It was the family thing again, I suspect; if I in any way could help them
to carry on, then in no way could I let the old firm down. As it turned out
I could play in everything they asked me to except Sorcerer, as I had a
previous engagement in Los Angeles. It was good to return to the
Company and things were as if I had never been away. The nights
I played were the same too: friends popped into my dressing room to
wish me luck, my stage ''Mum" Beti Lloyd-Jones, a chorister and
understudy of over 25 years standing, visited my dressing room to do
her duties - fastening my collar in Iolanthe, kissing me and wishing me
'Good luck, son,'.

My visits to the Adelphi spread over a month or so, during which time,
to my knowledge, none of the cast or other departments of the company
other than the management knew whether or not the D'Oyly Carte was
to live or die. The management did not know either. They, I presume,
were struggling to see if anything could be done to save the disaster which

eventually befell them: they could no longer see their way to carry on, and it seems it was only days before that I realized the family was to be broken up.

So came the ''Last Night,'' the true finale for the D'Oyly Carte Opera Company. It was to leave thousands of devoted fans saddened by the terrible news. Naturally there was the same rush to obtain seats for this last evening with their beloved Company, but for an entirely different reason. The last matinee, which was depressing enough, was to be H.M.S. Pinafore; and so I was to play their last full opera, for the evening performance was more in concert form with excerpts from all the operas from Trial by Jury to Grand Duke.

The evening itself could not have been sadder backstage, and indeed it was the same for practically the full audience I'm sure; people had arrived from all over, even from America. The show had to go on, nevertheless, as the old saying goes. There were newly hired costumes for the occasion. I was quite emotionally disturbed of course, as indeed were so many of the others, which all goes to make my memory of that night rather vague; but I do remember the tears of many, even a very tough stagehand who was crying quite openly.

That ever increasing and decreasing family is no more. The very last night typified the whole thing, the final curtain rising and then falling on an empty stage leaving everyone on both sides of the footlights, unbelieving and bewildered. That family was mine for thirty years, for although I had left them two and a half years before, I had not really gone. A true leader of the company who had ever belonged and lived through these touring days and theatres never did truly leave. I was no different than those that had played before and have gone since.

The final curtains went on and on, it seemed, until the last one finally stayed up. We all took more bows and then ignored the people out front, turned to one another, and hugged, kissed, said farewell, and at last in ones and twos and groups left the stage: it could be borne no more. The stage was at last empty with the curtain still up. The curtain never came down on that grand old Company. Goodbye, dear D'Oyly Carte.

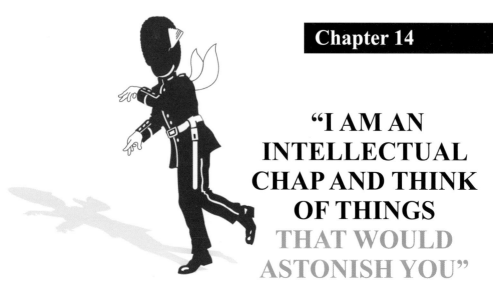

Chapter 14

"I AM AN INTELLECTUAL CHAP AND THINK OF THINGS THAT WOULD ASTONISH YOU"

Ian Smith's Memories

So what are my memories. I could probably write a book on those alone. The first time I saw him perform in Manchester. I wanted to go back and back and back. I was playing "his" roles and I wanted to watch his every movement, every nuance. I would take a lib with me and in the dark wrote down everything he did. I swore under my breath if I went to a matinee and Isadore Godfrey had the audacity to cut an encore.

In 1975 I co-founded the West Yorkshire Savoyard Appreciation Society. I think we fancied ourselves as the amateur equivalent to the D'Oyly Carte. We were amazingly ambitious. In those early days either myself or our Musical Director, James Newby, produced our shows. We thought nothing of doing "Pirates" and "Trial" on a Thursday; "The Mikado" on a Friday and "Iolanthe" on a Saturday – generally with the same cast.

I read somewhere that my idol, John Reed, was going to direct Harrogate Gilbert and Sullivan Society – only 20 miles away and proposed to the committee we invite him to come to Halifax to direct The Savoyards. Somehow I got the telephone number of Nicki's hotel in Bournemouth. John was away when I rang but Nicki suggested I went to see the show in Harrogate and he would arrange the meeting.

He did. A first face to face meeting. I don't know who was most excited – Jim Newby or myself. From the start John liked the idea of our group. We didn't rehearse for a month, produce for a week and then hibernate for the rest of the year. We rehearsed on and off all the year round. We had no base – we were indeed a group of strolling players.

Our next ambitious programme was a tour of Florida and we wanted John to direct us. There was an instant rapport. No haggling over fees. Yes he would be delighted. Our contract was a letter. £500 for a performance and "board and lodgings" with ME!

Amazing. He arrived and made himself totally at home. He was an easy house guest. Well I am not sure if easy is the right word. He was an insomniac – at night! After years of evening performances this was the time he came to life. Mornings were for sleeping! We would go to rehearsals; then off to the pub and back home. We both smoked like troopers. I had been directed earlier by Billy Morgan to whom John refers in the book; and Leslie Rands, Leonard Osborn, Mary Sansom and Ralph Mason. There was plenty to talk about. Night after night he recounted the humorous incidents of life on the road – and in the Carte! I wish I had had to sense to have recorded many of those conversations.

He was a superb cook. Beautiful light pastry and cakes; fabulous stew and dumplings - always waiting for me when I got home from the office. If he went home at the weekends he would leave post-it notes – don't forget this or that or the other. And when he went home at the end of the production I would continue to find these little post-it notes for weeks afterwards. "This is what you need to wash up!" "I belong in the cupboard!" "Don't forget to turn the lights off."

And what about the rehearsals. John was an extremely innovative director but he had a firm belief – if it isn't broken don't try to fix it. It fit in with precisely my own opinions of the G & S Operas. He emphasised that people should do their own thing. I suppose to an extent that particularly related to the roles I played because I wanted to be like him. But he reminded me time after time that he had not wanted to be a carbon copy of Peter Pratt. He had to bring himself to the parts.

John was sometimes a frustrated director. His own professional training

was self-evident. Punctuality, punctuality, punctuality! How could he start setting anything if half the chorus were missing. He experimented with principals. To some inflexible principals this could be frustrating as he would change moves from one rehearsal to another.
His reasoning was totally plausible. He needed to see how far he could take individuals.

His demonstration technique was something money could not buy. Those who wanted to learn could sit night after learn and watch his feet; his beautiful hand movements; his facial expression – it was like sitting in the audience at a D'Oyly Carte performance - only in close up.
I was not a good dancer – but John was the master of improvisation and we rehearsed and rehearsed simple moves that on film made me look like Nureyev!!

His encore materials were fantastic. Ko-Ko was perhaps my favourite part and he allowed me to use all his props. If they wore out I would arrive home from work and he had made another. Ingenious. Simple to operate – maximum effect to an audience of a hundred or several thousand. If he was with us during a run of performances he always insisted on making me up and the Katisha or Lady Jane.

Whenever we talked theatre or were in a theatre he was a man totally at ease with himself. Alive and alert.

He had a kind way of reminding you of the importance of Gilbert's words. Sometime he asked for a prompt of a particular line or phrase. Of course he never needed the prompt. It was a very clever and polite way of having you repeat the speech and if you repeated the mistake he would put his finger to his forehead and say – isn't it ....?
And of course it was.

In his eighties he was as light and nimble on his feet as someone sixty years younger. He had a grace and style of movement that you just loved to watch. And as a director he kept the very best of the tradition and introduced new business that fit perfectly.

A classic in my memory was the band he brought into The Sorcerer. What a simple yet effective addition. Providing he got contrasting shapes and sizes of bands people it really brought the house down.

Neil and I went to Boulder Colorado to see him at work with the University students. I visited New York as often as I could when he was performing with the New York Gilbert and Sullivan Players and I had a memorable trip to see him play Ko-Ko in a semi-staged production in Los Angeles. – "We'll have a party after the show." And we did. A handful of principals and musicians drove us into the Hollywood Hills for a magnificent roast beef dinner in the early hours.

The Savoyard Band

Of course there were so many other highlights. He was really thrilled to win the best Gilbert and Sullivan director at the Waterford International Festival of Light Opera and his productions helped us win more than 50 magnificent Waterford trophies in an eight year period.

The Waterford Trophies

With a young Neil Smith, this is John's final performance - Point at the Yeomen Centenary

The Savoyards group asked John if he would consider "playing" some of the roles. No hesitation – he would be delighted. Ko-Ko; Bunthorne, Sir Joseph and Jack Point came back to life. Point was his very last full scale performance appropriately played on the actual Centenary of the very first performance – October 3rd 1888. We wanted them to be special.

Jim Newby's wife suggested we looked at a "little Opera House in Derbyshire." We did and we played there with John in 1984 and again in 1985.

It was my introduction to the Buxton Opera House. I am quite sure that if we had not played there then the International Gilbert and Sullivan Festival might never have happened.

John instantly loved the theatre and years later when we were looking for a venue he was particularly enthusiastic for Buxton.

When the festival began we found ourselves one show short on a couple of occasions. That is how The Nomads was established. John just loved the Nomads and directed the three shows they presented in Buxton, Iolanthe, Sorcerer and Ruddigore. They were just great fun to be in. And what greater tribute to John than the fact that members of the cast travelled from South Wales, Scotland and South East of England at weekends – just to work with "the master."

John also directed the Gilbert and Sullivan Opera Company when health permitted. Regular visitors to Buxton pleaded for a "Patience" and we were thrilled when Anthony Besch who enjoyed a long and busy career as an opera director agreed to direct.

It was a brilliant spectacle – but it lacked humour, the basic essence of good Gilbert and Sullivan. The following year John accepted an invitation to put on a "humorous" Patience - and the audience loved every minute.

John's final stage performance - Together Again with Valerie, Ken and Tom

John "starred" in our two "Together Again" programmes in the Buxton Opera House when we brought back members of his beloved D'Oyly Carte family. His eyesight had failed so badly at the time of the second programme that he would only agree to go on stage if he could hold onto the arms of Neil and myself. But of course the old trooper spirit appeared and once he knew where he was he was off with his old mates – Ken, Tom and Valerie – in what was to be his very last stage appearance. And he loved every minute. John accepted he was getting older. It was a major frustration that he could no longer satisfy his insatiable creative appetite because of failing eyesight. He just loved visitors. That is when he really came to life – and if they could talk G & S so much the better. I was privileged to have worked with him on many productions. He worked with my son Neil and helped him develop characterisations for many of the "patter" roles. Twelve months ago I took my younger son Henry to have a Bunthorne lesson in preparation for the Buxton Youth Production. "No Henry – say it like this. Henry move your arms like this."
That was the last time we filmed him – "At Home with John Reed."
He was very frail.

John and Derrick

John often referred to the special stage relationship he had with Ken Sandford. I was fortunate to have a similar relationship in the Savoyards with Derrick Fuller and John directed my KoKo and his Pooh Bah or my Bunthorne and his Grosvenor on many occasions. Derrick died last Winter and John insisted on going to the funeral in Haworth Parish Church where the Rev. Patrick Bronte was the curate from 1820 and the Brontes are buried. It was a bitterly cold day. John and Nicki sat and enjoyed the old Savoyards rehearsing the very moving "Angelus" from Wallace's Maritana.

At the end of the service John was taken ill and spent the night in hospital. And that was really the beginning of the end of 94 happy and eventful years. Fifty two of them were spent with his special friend, his business advisor and partner, Nicki; and more than 70 of them entertaining hundreds of thousands of theatre goers around the world; teaching and passing on his skills to thousands of amateurs . Of one thing we can be quite sure – there will never be another John Reed OBE.

Chapter 15

"SURELY NEVER HAD A MALE SO ADVENTUROUS A TALE"

Article/interview on John Reed by Sandy Rovner:

"Behold the Lord High Comic of the Company; John Reed, O.B.E.; Dapper Interpreter"

Washington Post, April 9, 1978. In the Style section, p. F1.

IT IS ENTIRELY plausible to believe that John Reed is a figment of W.S. Gilbert's implausible imagination.

And John Reed, O.B.E., aka: Sir Joseph Porter, K.C.B., Ko-Ko, Jack Point, John Wellington Wells, the Lord Chancellor, Major General Stanley, King Gama, the Duke of Plaza-Toro, Reginald Bunthorne, Robin Oakapple and one or two others, the designated "principal comedian" of the D'Oyly Carte Opera Company, does nothing at all to dispel the illusion.

Indeed, sipping at a Scotch and ginger ale (warm) and nibbling at a plate of sausage and cheeses (cold), he says, at various times, of Jack Point (Yeomen of the Guard). "He's so me ." Of Ko-Ko (Mikado): "He's so me ." And of Bunthorne (Patience): "He's so me ."

And so he is essentially indistinguishable from the characters he has played for some 26 years now, this slight, mercurial, affable, sentimental, leprechaun of a man with his only-just-beginning-to-gray, only-just-beginning-to-thin curly red hair, his deep blue eyes, his chuckle and his sigh and his use of "dear" almost as a comma in a very near nonstop patter song of an interview.

"Yes," he concedes, his eyes twinkling - they twinkle a lot, even behind the glasses he wears offstage - "I'm the daddy of them all," the veteran of the company, for the past quarter-century or so the acknowledged master of the uniquely Gilbert and Sullivan patter song, the definitive interpreter of the tragi-comic, hilariously funny, painfully human, outrageous, forlorn and infinitely lovable characters who wend their singular ways through the operas of Gilbert and Sullivan.

"Oh, I'm very nervous, dear," he says when he's asked how he keeps these characters fresh night after night after night. Then he says, very fast: "Ooh, yes, I'm very highly strung. I'm nervous. It's not pleasant for me but I can't help it. After all this time I just take it. It always comes back to just one word: Caring. I really care. I care for my own pride in the performance, I suppose, and I care for the audience. All I want to do is please people so I do my utmost for them. Really, that's what I do it for. I do encores until I drop if they want me to."

An Accident

It was all something of an accident, the extraordinary union of John Reed and the D'Oyly Carte Opera Company. "I had no idea what this D'Oyly Carte thing was at all," says Reed. He'd been acting and producing in a repertory company - just straight acting, no musicals. A friend heard the D'Oyly Carte was looking for an understudy-chorister and told him about it. "Learn the Nightmare Song (lolanthe)," the friend had advised.

"Well," recalls Reed, "memorizing didn't seem much for someone in a repertory company," and that, to all intents and purposes was that. He hadn't even seen one of the productions.

So I thought I'd better go along and see what this D'Oyly Carte is, anyway," and he saw "The Gondoliers."

When he learned he'd won the part, "in a weak moment," he recalls, "I said yes. If I'd stopped to think I'd 'ave said, 'I can't do that. What am I doing going into an opera company? I'm not a singer.' I never professed to be a singer.

"Yes, but dancing. I've always danced ever since I could remember. Tap and Ballroom - I have medals for ballroom - and a slight bit of ballet. It always stood me in good stead because for these particular parts you don't have to be the world's best actor or the world's best dancer. But you have to have an accumulation of the whole thing." He paused. Sipped at his warm Scotch. "Above all," (twinkling again) "above all, you must be dapper. And small. If you're that, and you've got the other things slightly, well then you have the finished article."

John Reed is dapper, certainly, and small (5 feet 7) and though he complains that he's finding his costumes are getting a bit snug, his acrobatics and antics on stage belie any "slightness" to his dancing skills, and if he doesn't admit to the professionalism of his singing now, he's the only one, and, of course, his acting tops off the "accumulation" that could make him the Gilbert and Sullivan lead of all time.

"But," he sighs, wishing, he says, that all the old performances could have been "in the can" like old films, "while you're living, dear, you're never as good as the old ones. Not until I leave will anybody think that we've really done anything."

'Good Luck, Son'

Reed grew up in the north of England, county Durham, where his father was a butcher ("they slaughtered their own in those days, you know"). His parents and one of his three sisters have died, and he has never married. He is devoted to his two sisters, but the company is his family as well.

He's always had "a mum" in the company, ever since a contralto in the chorus told him she thought he'd been "so cute" when, as understudy, he'd gone on for an ailing Ko-Ko. "You were so cute I wanted to mother you," she told him. "So I said 'be my mum' and that's what she became," says Reed. "And it's been handed down - when she left - it had to be a contralto - and somebody else took over. For the past 16 years or so it's been Beti Lloyd-Jones. Never a night, not one night since then that she doesn't come to my dressing room and kiss me and say, 'Good luck, son." "That's what I mean," he says softly, "about the family thing."

Savoring the Feeling

Reed was pleased with the Kennedy Center audience reaction to the Lord Chancellor's Nightmare Song the other night, and, during the interview, just after the performance of Iolanthe, he was still savoring it. (Performances of "Mikado," "Pirates of Penzance," "Princes Ida" and "Pinafore" fill out the company's four-week stay here.)

"Sometimes you can't feel the reaction," he says. "In some theaters it doesn't come up to you, but tonight I felt it. What is so very pleasant is they're laughing at different places, mainly, and a little more. Perhaps it's because English audiences are used to it, know what's coming next. "Tonight," he says gleefully, "they were taking little points out of the songs . . ."

Reed has little trouble with the patter songs, he says. ("Oh, touch wood! Mind you each time I say this, it could happen tomorrow night.") But he concedes some are "harder to get your tongue around than others." "Nightmare," he notes, has a kind of continuity, a sort of story line. A killer is John Wellington Wells' song from "The Sorcerer." "Just a list of words" notes Reed, "now that is difficult. Nothing leads you to the next one. You could put them in any shape or form if you lost the rhythm," and then, in perfect rhythm, faster than a blink, he breaks into "changes organity/with an urbanity/full of Satanity/vexes humanity" and "barring tautology/in demonology/'lectro biology/mystic nosology/spirit philology/high-class astrology.

"It's a strange thing," says Reed, "I suppose after all this time, because my brain goes like this, I can be singing the 'Nightmare Song' and knowing what I'm singing, and at the same time I'll think, 'Oh, that poor woman in the audience, she can't see a thing because that woman's hat in front is too big.' That's what goes through my mind while I'm singing the song."

Reed was honored by the queen last year. But, he acknowledges, it was "a bit of a disappointment." "I went to the palace, of course, (for his Order of the British Empire) and I suppose it was all very pleasant. Everybody was dressed up and I was done up like a penguin. The uniforms were there. She's surrounded (Queen Elizabeth) by yeomen of the guard and she has this little, tiny simple blue dress on, a short blue dress, no jewelry. And I would like to have seen a tiara, I think, or something." He sighs.

Traditional. But not so traditional that he won't keep a bit of creeping American TV commercial out of a production. "We're amused by commercials on television. Last time we were here it was 'shyke and byke and ay'll hayelp.'" "'Sha-yke' and 'Ba-yke' and 'Hayelp,'" he repeats. "Something like that gets around the company." So much so that it's made it into "Gondoliers." "Do you have any sha-yke and ba-yke?" asks the Duke of Plaza-Toro (Reed) of a waiter. Well, it breaks up the company, anyway.

Chapter 16

"HIS CAPACITY FOR INNOCENT ENJOYMENT, IS JUST AS GREAT AS ANY HONEST MAN"

A Master Craftsman

Front page cover story in "Needlecraft" Magazine

He is a master craftsman. Whether his audience is captivated by his nimble tongue spitting out the most delightfully British Gilbert & Sullivan patter songs, or applauding his innovative and creative productions, John Reed OBE is still acknowledged to be the doyen of Gilbert & Sullivan both here in Britain and overseas.

But today he has developed another love – machine knitting; and as one might expect of a craftsman, he has taken tremendous pride in perfecting a hobby which has seen such a dramatic growth in popularity since John bought his first machine three years ago.

I am sure that many members of the club, like myself, will remember, with both pleasure and nostalgia, the tremendous versatility of John Reed during his 28 years with the now sadly missed D'Oyly Carte Opera Company.

needle crafts

the club for people who like fashion and making thin

From the lovable Ko-Ko one night to the delightful caricature of the Duke of Plazatoro the next; from the fleshly poet Bunthorne to the disagreeable King Gama, John Reed romped through his repertoire with the D'Oyly Carte night after night, from Edinburgh to Plymouth, from Manchester to Chicago to Sydney. Wherever he went he developed a most tremendous following of fans – loyal to this day. Not bad for the butcher's son from Darlington who left the D'Oyly Carte 9 years ago to 'try his hand at other things'. Try his hand he did, but you could say Gilbert & Sullivan was so entrenched in his blood that he didn't move all that far away. His new-found freedom, however, enabled him to experiment with the parts and to use his fantastic experience in producing and directing university students in Boulder, Colorado, enthusiastic amateurs in Brussels, Halifax, Harrogate and New York, and the semi-professionals in Los Angeles and Plymouth.

I know because I am one of the enthusiastic amateurs John directs here in Yorkshire, and it was probably in my home that he first unpacked his new 'toy'. He was directing at the time – but with amateurs this involves evening rehearsals, with lots of free time during the day.

Walking through Leeds he saw his knitting machine being demonstrated. He was quite startled to see how quickly the knitting grew and on impulse bought one – lock, stock and ribber. It's now become a way of life. John took the machine home, unpacked it, sorted it out, set it up, and away he went, it quickly became compulsive. As the machine yarn supplier benefitted, his local video library suffered. The television was switched off. Meals became secondary. Cups of tea went cold and he did not have as much time to smoke as he set about studying, practising and correcting his mistakes.

Indeed the more mistakes he made, the more he learnt and today, three years later, he wields his machine as adroitly as his fan in 'The Mikado'.

John rarely uses the patterns which so many suppliers provide. He knows what he wants and usually creates the designs in his mind and now punches out his own cards. Generally he uses wool rather than acrylic yarns, as he feels wool tends to be warmer, keeps its shape and washes and wears well.

He has found 'the extras', available with his machine particularly useful, and literally purchases any and every new attachment that the manufacturer supplies, from the intarsia carriage to lace carriage, from colour changer to a knit copy. He finds they save him time and the garments look tidier and more professional when they are finished. John knits for relaxation. During performances or productions, tension and adrenalin flow freely. Machine knitting is his therapy when he gets home. He knits purely for pleasure – principally for himself – but he gets as much pleasure giving a sweater to a friend as from receiving a standing ovation at the Royal Festival Hall. Much of his success is attributable to the books that have accumulated on his shelves relating to machine knitting. As he has developed a compulsion for the new extras for his machine so he has a mania to buy every book he sees.

One of his most exciting recent projects was to design and produce a wedding dress for one of his 'leading ladies' in America. His magnificent outfit is now completed entirely to his own design using a fine lace stitch. This was probably his most challenging project but the result was enormously satisfying.

We suggested to John that machine knitting was predominantly a hobby for women – did he feel in any way out of place? 'Absolutely not', he told us. 'In fact I would say machine knitting is as much a man's hobby. The knitting machine is a mechanical item. Today's machines are now incorporating electronics and computers which I think a man can understand as well as a woman'.

What effect has machine knitting had on his life? 'There is no doubt it has made me a much more patient human being. At one time if something went wrong I would have taken it off the machine and started again. Now I accept the challenge of sorting out the problem and doing the task thoroughly'.

After 28 years of touring the world with the D'Oyly Carte Opera Company, John Reed was accustomed to carrying his kettle, teapot and tea bags with him. Today his most important luggage items are his knitting machine and cones of yarn. He really knows his machine and understands exactly how each piece works. In addition to preparing for this season's productions he is now looking round the market to change the machine to keep up to date with the improved technologies that have made machine knitting so popular and successful in the United Kingdom. He certainly has "a song to sing-oh!" to support his new-found craft.

Chapter 17

"...ROBINSON CRUSOE WOULD JIB AT THEIR WEARING APPAREL"

John Reed as Castaway

On Saturday 23rd September 1972, in the the B.B.C. radio programme "Desert Island Discs", the castaway was John Reed.

He explained that he would not enjoy the loneliness, as he loved the noise and hustle of a city, but the records he would be choosing would be those reminding him of the past. He started with the Rachmaninov Second Piano Concerto, played by Vladimir Ashkenazy with the Moscow Philharmonic Orchestra, chosen for no reason except that he loved it; and he continued with "The Last Rose of Summer", sung by Ada Alsop, who came from his home town, Darlington, and whom he loved very dearly.

The next record, chosen because it was "my mood music. This is just what I would sit a long time and think about and remember," was Samuel Barber's Adagio for strings played by the strings of the Philadelphia Orchestra, conducted by Eugene Ormandy

The D'Oyly Carte Company went quite frequently to the United States and Canada, and had played one week in Copenhagen. He described the reception there as follows: - "They were delightful. I was so glad that I was warned that on the first night they give you a slow hand clap, and of course in England you'd think you were getting the bird or something, but you've got to expect this. Flowers were handed up to me as well as everybody else, and of course this would never happen in England - you'd get all the chorus boys sniggering! The third night comes, and if you don't get that slow hand clap and you don't get that bouquet of flowers you think, "What's happened here?"

His fourth record was the opening of the Pineapple Poll Ballet Suite, with Charles Mackerras conducting the Royal Philharmonic Orchestra, which he chose because he thought it had "that touch of everything" ---and reminded him of "people that have come and gone that I'd loved very dearly".

After mentioning the film of "The Mikado" and the backing the Company did for the "Ruddigore" cartoon - he enjoyed making the film but didn't like it when he saw it - John Reed went on to discuss the running-out of the Gilbert and Sullivan copyrights in 1961. He thought that the competitive productions which had been set up had seemed to make no difference; the D'Oyly Carte performances seemed as popular as ever. He hoped to stay with the Company, as he was very happy there and the Company was just like a family-differences and all!

For his fifth record he chose "Little Cloud", from Offenbach's "La Vie Parisienne", sung by Cynthia Morey and Eric Shilling with the Sadler's Wells Opera Company. Besides the similarity of Offenbach with Gilbert and Sullivan, this choice was made because Cynthia was his very first friend in the D'Oyly Carte Company, and was still his dearest friend; he actually lived in the same street now. He was a great fan of Eric Shilling, even though the latter played his parts in the Sadler's Wells Opera Company.

For his sixth record, he chose "The Stripper", played by David Rose and his orchestra. This was to remind him of America and the Company's

American tours; it had the rush, the bustle, the burlesques - everything that would bring everything back to him. He was asked about his hobbies, and he said that his principal one was oil painting, though he was a handy man in many ways - he could make a basket, or a lampshade, or a pair of trousers, anything he wanted to make. He was also confident that he could run up a waterproof shelter on his desert island and could catch fish and cook it; he reckoned he was a very good cook. He would not try to escape from the island, because he would be afraid of the expanse of ocean, especially at night; he was sure someone would come to pick him up.

His last two records were a complete contrast to one another. For the seventh, he chose Richard Kiley and Irving Jacobson in the New York production of "Man of La Mancha". For the final one, he chose "Come Dance the Syrtaki", played by Stelios Zafirou, because he had loved his holidays in Greece so much and Greek music was such lovely holiday music.

Lastly, he was told he must decide which of his eight records, if he could take only one, he would choose; what luxury he would take; and what book, apart from the Bible and Shakespeare. His answers were the Rachmaninov; lots of canvases, oil paints, and brushes; and, because he rarely read books twice, a large book on 'Do It Yourself'.

Recordings

John recorded for Decca all his roles, some more than once. Memories can be refreshed by playing records at home. when one can recall his nuances of expression. It is for this reason that this appreciation has concentrated less on his considerable musicianship and more on his personality as an actor. The two, nevertheless, go together.
If unexpected joie de vivre breaks out at a London "Last Night" (as when in 1979 his Bunthorne had 'Barclays" tattooed on his chest), he has never forgotten that Gilbert and Sullivan are humorists of word and note, and he has been a great interpreter of both.

Chapter 18

"A TALE SO FREE FROM EVERY DOUBT
– ALL PROBABLE POSSIBLE SHADOW OF DOUBT"

Bernard Lee, then Arts Critic for the Sheffield Telegraph and another supporter of the Festival, profiled John in a series of articles back in 2001

"GENIUS WHO CAN TURN ON TEARS AND LAUGHTER"

Genius, it is said, cannot be defined.

John Reed, for many the foremost Gilbert and Sullivan patter man of all time, especially in his years with the original D'Oyly Carte Opera Company, would blush at being so called.

He is mild mannered with no airs and graces, off-stage at any rate. Robin Oakapple (Ruddigore) would be him, but not tetchy King Gama (Princess Ida), or egotistical Reginald Bunthorne (Patience).

That's when elements of genius come in. He was both to perfection, yet never lost sight of the fact that they are comic characters by giving them a sense of mischief which was at the core of all his performances of the G&S patter roles – KoKo (Mikado), Sir Joseph Porter (HMS Pinafore),

Jack Point (Yeomen of the Guard), Lord Chancellor (Iolanthe), Duke of Plaza-Toro (Gondoliers) and Major General Stanley (Pirates of Penzance) are also indelibly associated with John Reed. There was a certain quixotic quality about his playing of the roles too, even vulnerability which, while in a comic vein most of the time, was also tragic when he played Jack Point. "I'm a terribly sensitive and sympathetic person – always have been. I can cry at anything. Before I came on as Jack Point at the end (of Yeomen), all I had to do was think of something sad and come on.

"I would come on and cry through 'O thoughtless crew! You know not what you do. Shed a tear or two – I have a song to sing, O!

"There was one occasion, I remember it quite distinctly, when there was a matinee as well as evening performance of Yeomen, I thought 'I can't die twice in one day', so I put the glycerine tears on my eyes at the matinée.

"After the performance Beryl Dixon, a chorister then, came up, tears streaming down her face, and said: 'Oh, John! You really got it today'. I thought: 'That was the one time when I wasn't really crying'.

"After that, it was a mixture. You can't control the sobs when you're actually crying and you have to sob in the right place when you're singing. I still felt it, through the glycerine and real tears. I had just as much feeling about it. I could break my heart over somebody who didn't love me."

It was John's total identity with any part he was playing which endeared him to audiences all over the world, particularly in this country and America.

Even now, the affection he is held in is quite incredible.

Last year's Together Again concert (2000) in the Gilbert and Sullivan Festival in Buxton, when members of the original D'Oyly Carte appeared on stage for the first time since the company closed in 1982, provided overwhelming proof of that.

Thomas Round might have brought the house down doing a nimble hornpipe in his 85th year but John Reed, now 84, only had to walk on stage and the ovation was deafening.

If audiences adored John Reed, he had a strong attachment to them.

"I loved my audiences. I was so grateful to them, so grateful. You could get them to such a pitch. What could be better?

"There were the wonderful parts, tailor-made for anyone who could bring them off, and a ready-made audience longing for the music and longing for the laughter.

"I found in the encores I could just wink at the audience and they would fall apart because they were at such a pitch. That's delightful. What a reward it is!

"The encores were a bit of fun between me and the audience, especially with these parts. They were all different. You don't go back on stage and do the same thing again.

"In one of the encores after 'Never mind and why and wherefore' (Pinafore), I'd bring a fish out of my pocket and drop it into the orchestra pit. When I came out again they handed the bones back to me.

"I remember, one day, after six or seven encores of it, Isadore Godfrey (the conductor) signalled another. I had nothing ready, nothing set in my mind so I made something up, wriggled my bum or something.

"It made them laugh but I thought if that happens again, I'm going to have something ready. So I decided that I would jump overboard as if to say, 'oh, I've had enough of this'.

"Sure enough, it happened so I went to the back, nipped my nose and jumped overboard. The audience fell about – just fell about. The orchestra stopped playing to look what had happened and Goddie (Isadore Godfrey) practically fell off the box (podium)."

The business of a special touch

When John Reed first jumped overboard it achieved gospel-like status and became part of the 'business', often called tradition, in original D'Oyly Carte Opera Company productions.

That was how a lot of the so-called tradition came about, through innovation.

Another piece of business John introduced involving Sir Joseph Porter – the "Ruler of the Queen's Navee" who never went to sea – was to have him semaphore 'help'.

"I just waved my arms about but, when I went to a cocktail party at Admiralty House, I was introduced to the First Lord of the Admiralty. I said: 'You're just the man I want to know. Can you tell me how to say help in semaphore?

"He said: 'Oh, don't ask me, go and ask my commander over there', exactly as Gilbert wrote it.

"When I took over the patter roles from Peter Pratt, I found there was a lot of 'business', which just didn't suit me, Peter played Ko-Ko much different to me, as a solemn, down-trodden man. I played him with more mischief because that's my personality.

"Gradually, I changed things because of that, changed lots of encores, everything eventually, I suppose. What I found I was doing lots of the time was defying the company in a way and the tradition.

"I was a dancer and brought a lot of dancing to the parts because it suited me. I never confessed to being a singer. I used to say, they might not like my voice, but they're jolly well gong to hear me. To me it was like a play.

"A lot of the business developed through continuous working with the same people. There were all sorts of little things which we never spoke about. If we had, it would have ruined it.

John, in Buxton, with Kenneth Sandford

"You worked with these people so much, you only had to look in their eyes and know exactly what mood they were in, you looked in Ken Sandford's eyes on a particular day and knew it was his day for pregnant pauses, when he would pause a little longer than normal in the dialogue on stage.

"Ken was wonderful to work with. I used to think we were the Laurel and Hardy of Gilbert and Sullivan because I'm small and he's big."

Long before joining D'Oyly Carte, John had won awards for ballroom dancing in his native Darlington. He was the only son of a butcher and his first job was in a builder's office – 'Mr Bean, he was called,' smiles the later D'Oyly Carte legend.

He joined an amateur operatic group and was headhunted by the local repertory company to play juvenile leads on the strength of his entrances and exits.

"I was working with professional actors who didn't know I was just an amateur and they used to say to me, 'isn't it awful, these amateurs coming in and putting us out of work'."

An understudy's lot

The road to becoming a D'Oyly Carte legend started when the young John Reed joined the operatic group in his native Darlington and got to know a baritone called Eric Thornton.

Eric eventually left to join D'Oyly Carte Opera and a few years after that he met his brother, who revealed that the siblings had been talking about D'Oyly Carte's need for an understudy for the patter roles. The only person Eric's brother could think of was John Reed.

"He asked me if I would be interested and I said yes. Eric arranged an audition in Glasgow so I went, sang the Nightmare Song (Iolanthe), of all things, and Jack's the Boy for Me, went back to Darlington and thought, well, that's that.

"A week later I got a letter saying Bridget D'Oyly Carte was visiting the company in Edinburgh and she'd like to hear me. I went, did the same things again, and they asked me if I knew any dialogue.

"I remembered this mad scene I'd done so I acted away, ghostly howls and all, and there was a deathly hush after I'd finished. I thought, 'you've gone too far this time, mate.' Then a voice out of the dark said: 'We want you Mr. Reed, can you come?'

"By the time I'd got to the wings, they'd given me all the books. I'd never seen a Gilbert and Sullivan opera before, so I went back to the theatre and saw my first one that night."

He joined D'Oyly Carte as a chorus member and understudy to Peter Pratt in November 1951 and took over all the patter roles when Pratt left in 1959.

His presence, it would seem was soon felt, which may account for Peter Pratt's relatively short reign after the long ones of his illustrious predecessors Martyn Green and Henry Lytton.

"I never wanted to be a principal. I was very happy in the chorus because they were my friends. I didn't go in as a principal, I went in as an understudy.

"I was told I must ask at my interview for a show a week to keep in touch. So I did and they said they had to consider Mr. Pratt's position. In point of fact, they were going to let me go rather than do that.

"What happened was I would get a letter from Bridget saying: In your capacity as principal understudy we would like you to play Jack Point on such-and-such a night.

"Then I would get another letter to say Mr. Pratt had objected to my playing in such-and-such a performance, would I mind changing it?

"I remember, when he left, I said to him: 'I want to tell you something. I never wanted your parts, Peter, and you had no need to be afraid of me. I would have been your friend from the beginning if you'd allowed me, but you never did'.

John Reed's 28 years with the D'Oyly Carte Opera Company turned out to be its golden era.

"I like to think of it like that," he says. ''I can tell you something else. Suddenly, people were acting." That inevitable semi-circle, always with the girls in front and the boys behind, crumbled.

"Everything became natural, more believable. We weren't regulated, not so stilted. We began to believe what we were saying and the performances became much more intense."

Breaking down conceptions wasn't always easy, though.

"I remember going to rehearse the Duke of Plaza-Toro (Gondoliers) with Sir Malcolm Sergeant. I never agreed with him just conducting first nights in London when Isadore Godfrey was our music director and toured with us all the time."

"Anyway, he was sat at a piano, played the Duke's entrance and, when I opened my mouth to sing, he stopped and said: 'This used to be the most magnificent entrance once upon a time when Henry Lytton came on'.

"He started again and broke off again, and said: 'yes, it was magnificent'. After about six times I was getting a bit fed up and said: 'I'm sorry to say, Henry Lytton is dead and gone and you've got me and you haven't allowed me to open my mouth yet'.

He kept me back afterwards, and I thought, dear me, I'm going to get the cane. He said: 'Would you have a cup of tea with me, John, a glass of sherry, or something'. Nobody had challenged him before."

The things he had to put up with, even as the established star of the company, beggar belief. The more he talks about them, the more realisation dawns that management attitudes hadn't changed since Gilbert and Sullivan's time.

D'Oyly Carte performed 48 weeks a year which, in John's time as patter man, included seven tours to America and one each to Denmark, Rome and Australisia, as well as perpetual touring in the UK.

Virtually on every night and never getting one off, he wanted to give up Major General Stanley (Pirates), a part he didn't like very much. Eventually, he succeeded.

Soon after, a tour to America was put into jeopardy because the promoters wanted him to play all the patter parts. Asked to play just the press nights of Pirates as Major General Stanley, he agreed.

"The press nights were the only nights they played Pirates in America!"

Cheers!
"Major General" Reed

His weekly wage with D'Oyly Carte was £100 and £3 was what the understudy got if they went on.

It's amazing he stood for it for long.

"It's true. It applied to all of us really. I'll tell you why we did it. It was for love of the operas and love of one another. We were never classed as anything, there's umpteen things which upset you and should never have happened.

"For all that, everyone who was a member of the company refers to it as a family. We were. Everywhere we went, we made it our home. We took our hobbies with us. Neville Griffiths and his wife made wine. Ken Sandford and I dabbled in painting.

John and Sheba

"We took our pets with us. At one time, I had a boxer, Sheba. Pauline Wales had a Dalmatian and Jon Ellison toured with little water turtles, swishing about in a tank.

"You took as much of your home as you could because it was your life. It was a way of life. I don't think we would have had it any different.

"What we liked to do was get an apartment of our own. That's how cooking became one of my hobbies (he's an expert figurine-maker, too). It made life a little harder, I suppose, cooking for yourself, you'd get your luggage in and then go and do your shopping.

"In some ways, though, it had its advantages over digs. I remember the story of Meston Reid – do you remember Meston, a fine tenor. I never forgave him for having my name.

"He and some other company members got back to their digs late one night to find the landlady drunk. She greeted them saying 'loss the joint. I put it in the oven and I've loss the joint'. So they went to look for it.

"Sure enough, the gas was on and they looked in the oven, but no joint. Looking round, they noticed a cupboard under the sink. She'd put it in there."

John's point of no return

Awarded on OBE in 1976, John Reed left the D'Oyly Carte Opera Company in 1979. Its demise was swift and it closed in 1982.

"It was heart-breaking. It should never have happened. If they'd had a theatrical management, got a darned good director, moved with the times, they would still be going today.

"They were Victorian, stubborn and unbending. What more can I say about them?

"It's come back again, hasn't it? But it's not the same. They're all freelance. They go in, do the show and go off to do something else".

John's dismay at the closure of the original D'Oyly Carte is genuine, yet also hard to reconcile with the way he was treated when he told the company he was leaving. But that's the make-up of the man.

He doesn't particularly want the sordid, not to say petulant, details published but, briefly, he handed his notice in during the 17-week tour of Australasia in 1979.

He'd been thinking about it for a while but the "straw which broke the camel's back" was when the conductor, Fraser Goulding, asked the chorus to stay behind after an Iolanthe rehearsal for two minutes and the Equity representative said: "You know you'll be going into overtime, Mr. Goulding."

Two minutes! I came out with Jill Pert and said: 'That's it, Jill'. It's time I went. It didn't happen in my day, everyone was so conscientious, and the new ones coming in were different. It was just a job now.

He was hardly prepared for what followed. Just about the whole company stopped speaking to him.

"My last show was in Pinafore in Perth. I walked off to my dressing room alone, I took off my costume, I hung it up, put my hat and coat on and walked to my lodgings.

"I just don't know why they did it. Maybe they saw the beginning of the end. I didn't believe it and it took a lot of getting over. I liked to forget it actually."

He went back as a guest artist, though.

"Yes, I went back. They wrote and asked me if I'd do the final season. Even then, you know, it wasn't right. I heard people say things like, 'I don't believe in people coming back as guest artists now.'

"Valerie (Masterson) was going back. She did the same kind of thing. Valerie could rise above it, but I just couldn't – I couldn't. I was hurt."

And yet he was sorry when it went?

"Oh yes, of course. I didn't want it to go. These were my friends."

John is still sprightly. His health isn't wonderful and he's going blind in one eye.

He's never stopped – old D'Oyly Cartians never do, they just keep going – although he did think he'd thrown himself out of work after leaving D'Oyly Carte.

"Do you know, I didn't think anyone knew me, quite honestly. We were all just members of D'Oyly Carte in those days. As principals, we got no privileges.

"Soon after I left I got a letter from the University of Colorado, asking me if I would go and direct. They'd written to D'Oyly Carte and said was there anyone they could recommend to direct this show.

"They said John Reed has just left the company, why don't you try there. I said 'yes' and went over. I kept going there for 13 years. They were marvellous people and I had a wonderful time."

He directed and did some performing – always Gilbert and Sullivan- with companies in places like New York, Tulsa, Katona Beach and Cleveland. He is, actually, a very fine director of G&S.

He began directing amateurs in this country, becoming great friends with Ian Smith, chairman of the West Yorkshire Savoyards in Halifax, where he has finally settled after years of living out of a suitcase.

When Ian started the Gilbert and Sullivan Festival in Buxton eight years ago, John happily agreed to be its president, although ill health caused him to miss the odd year or two.

It's given him the chance to meet old friends from the original D'Oyly Carte who he "misses terribly" again: Kenneth Sandford, Gillian Knight, Jean Hindmarsh, Valerie Masterson and Thomas Round.

He must have played parts like Ko-Ko, Sir Joseph Porter and Jack Point thousands of times, night after night, how did he manage to keep them fresh?

"Because I'm very highly strung, eager to please, it was my job, and I wanted to do a good job.

"There's a million reasons. As I've already said, I loved my audience. I always wanted to try things out that were different, to try and get more out of the part.

"I'm always being asked which was my favourite one, which one I enjoyed most, and I say the one I was playing on a particular night and there's a hell of a lot of truth in it.

"I identified strongly with Jack Point, I suppose, because he was a strolling player like me, but all the parts are wonderful and all different. They have such pearls of wisdom.

"If I could be young, if I could go back, God! Could I play those parts now, I'm still young inside."

Chapter 19

"HAIL FLOWING
FOUNT
OF SENTIMENT"

John Reed (actor)

The Entry in Wikipedia, the free web-based, collaborative multilingual encyclopedia.

John Lamb Reed, OBE (13 February 1916 – 13 February 2010) was an English actor, dancer and singer, known for his nimble performances in the principal comic roles of the Savoy Operas, particularly with the D'Oyly Carte Opera Company. Reed has been called "the last great exponent" of the Gilbert and Sullivan comedy roles.

The son of a butcher from County Durham, Reed began performing at the end of World War II, joining the D'Oyly Carte Opera Company in 1951. After eight years as understudy to Peter Pratt, he became the principal comedian of the company in 1959, remaining for two decades, playing all the

John Reed as Ko-Ko;   Kenneth Sandford as Pooh Bah

famous Gilbert and Sullivan patter roles, including Sir Joseph in H.M.S. Pinafore, the Major-General in Pirates, Bunthorne in Patience, the Lord Chancellor in Iolanthe, Ko-Ko in The Mikado, Jack Point in The Yeomen of the Guard and the Duke of Plaza Toro in The Gondoliers, among others. He was known for his "fleet-footed clowning", dry and roguish wit, comic timing, "crystal clear diction" in the patter songs, and his amusing character voice, recording all of his principal roles with the company.

In 1979, Reed left the company but continued performing in and directing Gilbert and Sullivan productions in Britain and America, as well as appearing in other light opera. He retired to Halifax, West Yorkshire, directing amateur Gilbert and Sullivan companies and attending the International Gilbert and Sullivan Festival in Buxton for many years.

Life and career

Reed was born in the village of Close House, near Bishop Auckland, County Durham, the fourth and youngest child of Robert Elliott Reed, a butcher (b. 1874) and his wife, Elizabeth Ann, nee Bridges (b. 1883) "an excellent amateur soprano who rescued the family finances by opening a successful fish shop" after his father's butcher shop failed. He was named after his grandfather, a Wesleyan Methodist minister. His sisters were Christina (b. 1903), Betty (b. 1905) and Anne "Hannah" Reed Hunter (b. 1912) (a younger brother, Cyril, died in infancy). Reed played the piano as a child. From age eleven, he grew up near the much larger town of Darlington, County Durham. He studied elocution, dancing, singing and mime, but worked in builders' and insurance offices. During World War II, he enlisted in the auxiliary fire service and worked as an instrument maker.

Reed began his theatrical career, after the war, in plays with a repertory theatre company, and as a dancer, winning medals for dance across the North-East of England. When his father became ill, he returned home to work in his father's business, and performed in musical theatre for a number of years with local amateur companies including the Darlington Operatic Society. He was also a director and dance instructor for the Darlington Education Committee.

D'Oyly Carte years

Reed joined the D'Oyly Carte Opera Company in 1951 as the understudy to Peter Pratt, who had recently become the principal comedian of the company. At the time of his audition, he knew little or nothing about Gilbert and Sullivan, but company manager, Frederic Lloyd, assured him that the company preferred this so that they could "start you off in the way we mean you to go". The company performed 48 weeks per year, mostly on tour, usually with winter seasons in London. Reed appeared in the chorus and was given several smaller roles: Associate (1952–55) in Trial by Jury, Major Murgatroyd in Patience (1952–59), Second Citizen in The Yeomen of the Guard (1952–59), Annibale (1952–59) and Antonio (1953–59) in The Gondoliers (a role that took advantage of his dancing skills), and Mr. Cox in Cox and Box (1957–59). He was coached in his own roles and those he understudied by Eleanor Evans, the company's stage director. In 1955, Reed began to play the Learned Judge in Trial. He also substituted for Pratt occasionally, including when Pratt was ill in March and April 1959.

In 1959, when Pratt left the D'Oyly Carte Opera Company, Reed became the principal comedian, remaining in that role for the next twenty years. Writer Andrew Lamb noted that Reed's "nimble dancing, characterful light-baritone singing, and the business he was able to introduce into encores and elsewhere within the generally rigid D'Oyly Carte constraints, soon helped to establish his own loyal following, and the personal rapport he enjoyed with his fans grew to legendary status." During these two decades, his parts were as follows: Sir Joseph Porter in H.M.S. Pinafore, Major-General Stanley in The Pirates of Penzance (a role that he gave up in 1969), Bunthorne in Patience, the Lord Chancellor in Iolanthe, King Gama in Princess Ida, Ko-Ko in The Mikado, Robin Oakapple/Sir Ruthven in Ruddigore, Jack Point in The Yeomen of the Guard, the Duke of Plaza-Toro in The Gondoliers, and John Wellington Wells in The Sorcerer (beginning with the 1971 revival). He dropped from his repertory the role of the Judge in Trial by Jury, in 1959, briefly resuming it for the D'Oyly Carte's centenary celebrations at the Savoy Theatre in 1975. For that season, he also played Scaphio in Utopia,

Limited and Grand Duke Rudolph in the company's concert of The Grand Duke. The company had not performed these two works since the original productions in the 1890s. Reed also participated in eleven of the company's overseas tours to North America (eight times), Denmark (1970), Rome (1974) and Australia and New Zealand (1979).

In 1977, Reed was honoured as an Officer of the Order of the British Empire (OBE). He played before Queen Elizabeth II and other members of the Royal Family at least eight times, including in 1977 for the Queen's Silver Jubilee Command Performance, at Windsor Castle, of H.M.S. Pinafore. Reed told interviewer Colin Prestige that "When the Prince of Wales, aged eleven, saw The Mikado, Ko-Ko afterwards entertained him in the dressing-room." Although Reed loved the family atmosphere of the company during his nearly thirty years there, he later felt that the company's dynamic was changing. He decided to leave the company during the 1979 Australasian tour, and author Ian Bradley relates one of the incidents that served as a tipping point: "At the end of their first rehearsal [in Australia], conductor Fraser Goulding asked the chorus to stay on for a few minutes just to polish the act 2 finale. The Equity representative promptly stood up and said, 'You know that means we'll be going into overtime'. Reed says: ... we used to go on far into the evening working on things to get them right and never thought of overtime. I realized that was the time to go'."

A specially commissioed plate commemorating the award of his OBE

Assessment

Reed said that, of all the Gilbert and Sullivan roles, he probably best loved Ko-Ko, noting, "Ko-Ko is almost me. There's a lot of me in the character. It lets me bring out my sense of humour and delivery of lines.... [In] the character parts ... you must get your own personality through." On the other hand, Reed said, "Something takes over from me when I go on. I become something different. I'm basically shy, and I go and hide behind my characters."

He also said of Ko-Ko, "it's such fun to do... you make people laugh, and the children and everybody enjoy him. And I suppose that's what our job is here anyway. To entertain people."

Reed also loved to play Jack Point in Yeomen, a tragicomic character. "Jack Point is me in another age – just a strolling player. I really believe I could die of a broken heart". Reed said that every comedian savours the chance to play a role like Point in which "you like to see if you can make 'em cry a little".

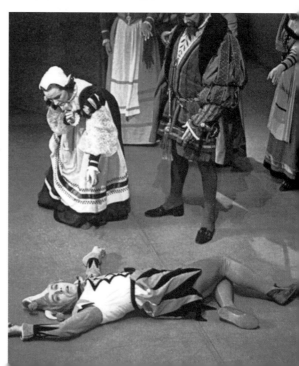

He also noted that, generally, "I like anything where the dancing comes in". His least favourite role was Major-General Stanley in Pirates, a role that he gave up in 1969. He also found two drawbacks to playing King Gama: "the heavy make-up ... hid every feature of his face except his eyes, and made it impossible for him to wear his glasses so that he could do his newspaper crossword while waiting to go on". Of the "younger" roles he played even in his later years with the company, Reed said, "I feel I'm so fundamentally a young person.... I'm older than the part I'm playing, for instance, but I feel young."

Two Lord Chancellor's - Lord Hailsham and "Lord" John Reed

He loved performing for children and delighted in the gala "last nights" of each London season with the D'Oyly Carte, where he would perform for glittering audiences of "Prime Ministers, Lord Chancellors and First Lords of the Admiralty."

In its obituary, The Guardian asserted: Reed's "comic timing, nimble footwork and clarity of diction made him the acknowledged master of the "patter" roles, at once the most challenging and defining of all Gilbert and Sullivan's creations".

His biographer, Cynthia Morey, praised his "feet that hardly seemed to touch the floor as he danced across the stage; the sly glance and raised eyebrow that could bring the house down."

The Times called his stage personality "impish", writing: "He was, quite simply, a phenomenon. For 48 gruelling weeks of each of those 20 years he effortlessly negotiated the tongue-twisting patter songs." The latter paper judged Reed a success in his desire to play pathos: "His Jack Point, the lovelorn jester in The Yeomen of the Guard, and the role which he dubbed 'the one apart, the Hamlet of Gilbert and Sullivan', could easily bring a tear to the eye, as did his spoken rendition of 'Iolanthe, thou livest?'" Of his Ko-Ko, The Times stated, "The brightest performance of the evening comes from Mr. John Reed, a spirited Ko-Ko with exactly the right stature and crystal clear diction". The same paper commented, regarding his Sir Joseph Porter, "Mr. Reed's impersonation, prim, dry, roundly articulated (and sung in tune, as some of his illustrious predecessors never attempted to do), was eminently likeable." Of his Sir Ruthven Murgatroyd, it said, "Reed, in particular, chose understatement as his main weapon, and in his dryness, at once naive and sophisticated, produced a Murgatroyd very much in the authentic D'Oyly Carte tradition. Critic Alan Blyth commented that in his Bunthorne,"Reed ... remains a past master of keeping the text fresh and articulated". Blyth also wrote that "The Lord Chancellor is one of John Reed's most appropriate roles, with plenty of scope for his fleet-footed clowning, and in the Nightmare-Song he gives an object-lesson in projecting one of Gilbert's most complex texts."

Reed's fans eagerly anticipated his "business" in the many encores that followed some of his songs, in which "his antics would become ever more outrageous.... Reed's Sir Joseph Porter would jump overboard only to re-enter clutching a rubber life-ring, while ... his Ko-Ko would be found furiously – and anachronistically – pedalling across the stage in a toy car." On the other hand, he was sometimes criticized for these instances of dropping character and adding anachronisms. He explained,"An encore is a different thing – a bit of fun between me and the audience – then I come right back into character again."

After the D'Oyly Carte

After he left the D'Oyly Carte organisation in 1979, Reed continued to perform in, and direct, Gilbert and Sullivan productions for the rest of his career, also occasionally appearing in other theatre. He appeared as a guest artist numerous times with D'Oyly Carte after his retirement, including their "last night" concert. The solo show A Song to Sing O was created for and premiered by him at the Savoy Theatre in 1981. The reviewer for The Times disliked the piece, commenting, "The attraction is almost entirely the talented twisting of Mr. Reed's tongue around familiar patter."

Reed performed and directed, through the 1980s, with many Gilbert and Sullivan companies, both professional and amateur, flying back and forth from Europe to North America. These theatre companies included the Brussels Gilbert and Sullivan Society, the CU Opera Company in Boulder, Colorado (which awarded him an honorary doctorate)

and the Colorado Music Theatre Festival there, and The Lyric Opera of Dallas. In 1983, he performed as Menelaus in Offenbach's La belle Hélène, and in a double bill of Trial by Jury (as the Learned Judge) and Offenbach's M. Choufleuri (as M. Balandard), with the Washington Opera at the Kennedy Center. He continued to direct in the U.S. into the early 1990s.

Buxton Opera House, where Reed appeared at our Gilbert and Sullivan Festival in later years.

He appeared, from 1984 until 1989, with the New York Gilbert and Sullivan Players (NYGASP), earning warm reviews for his "subtle facial gesture and small comic touch" and clear diction. Of his 1986 Bunthorne with the company, The New York Times wrote, "Mr. Reed does not overdo. He sings and speaks in a moderate tone of voice, never moves more than fairly quickly, and never hits the audience over the head with a joke. As a result, when he strikes a pose of even mild ridiculousness, the result is hilarity. He makes Bunthorne a good-natured poseur, and admits his dependency on adulation with endearing simplicity." At a NYGASP gala at Symphony Space in 1987, Reed proposed on stage to noted sex therapist Dr. Ruth Westheimer. He also performed in concerts in North America and Britain, including at The Berkshire Choral Institute as The Duke of Plaza Toro (with Kenneth Sandford as Don Alhambra) in The Gondoliers (1985). In reviewing a 1988 concert, the The Boston Globe wrote that Reed "is near to perfect in his chosen field. Reed's acting, his command of patter and everything he does (which is a lot) to convince you that what he's emitting could really be mellifluous, all-out singing – all these are freshly and tirelessly amusing".

After retiring from the stage, Reed moved to Halifax, West Yorkshire, England, with his partner (since 1958) John Nicholas Kerri, who also acted as his business manager. There he directed local amateur Gilbert and Sullivan societies, including the Harrogate Gilbert and Sullivan Society (1980–1994) and the West Yorkshire Savoyards, among others. Reed continued to direct until at least 2004, including productions at the International Gilbert and Sullivan Festival, where he also gave talks and participated in events, often with other former members of the D'Oyly Carte. Neil Smith, a director of that Festival, commented, "Reed had an unrivalled ability to imbue his performances with both madcap humour and deep pathos, a quality which, combined with the acrobatic agility of a trained dancer, brought him worldwide acclaim."

Throughout his life, Reed had many hobbies, including oil painting, crafts and cooking, and he loved the ballet. He published his autobiography, Nothing Whatever to Grumble At: His Story, as told to Cynthia Morey, in 2006.

Reed died on 13 February 2010 at the Calderdale Royal Hospital, Halifax, England, on his 94th birthday, after suffering from a stroke. He had lost most of his eyesight through macular degeneration and had been diagnosed with dementia just before Christmas 2009. Reed's remains were cremated, after a funeral service on 23 February, at Park Wood Crematorium, Elland.

Recordings

John Reed recorded all of his major roles with the D'Oyly Carte Opera Company for Decca Records between 1960 and 1979, some of them twice, and several of them complete with dialogue. In 1976, he participated in the only D'Oyly Carte recordings of Utopia, Limited and The Grand Duke, playing, respectively, Scaphio and Grand Duke Rudolph. These recordings are still available either on the Decca label or under licence from Decca on Sounds on CD, a private label specialising in Gilbert and Sullivan recordings. Reed also appeared in the 1967 film version of The Mikado and the 1973 video of H.M.S. Pinafore as Ko-Ko and Sir Joseph Porter, respectively. A 1965 BBC television broadcast of Patience with Reed as Bunthorne is apparently lost. He was also the voice of Robin Oakapple in the 1967 Halas and Batchelor Ruddigore cartoon.

Chapter 20

"Is life a Boon?
If so it must befall
That Death whene'er he call
must call too soon!"

"PARAGRAPHS
GOT INTO
ALL THE PAPERS"

Neil Smith's announcement

I'm very sad to report that at 02.00am GMT today,
13th February John Reed passed away peacefully in the
Calderdale Royal Hospital, Halifax. It was his 94th birthday.

Many will know that John had been suffering from ill health
for some time. Last week he was re-admitted due to a
stroke, from which he never recovered.

Goodbye dear John - thanks for the memories.

John Reed February 13th 1916 - February 13th 2010

The announcement of the death of John Reed spread round the world within minutes. A "FACEBOOK" tribute page was established where some moving tributes and unseen pictures were posted. Impatience was expressed at the time it took the national papers at home and abroad to recognise the closing of one of Gilbert and Sullivan's most important chapters. But patience was rewarded and alongside the very individual comments came those from very significant theatre critics.......

"British baritone John Reed (alias Ko-Ko, Major-General Stanley, and other disguises), in true Gilbert & Sullivan style, deferred to the Lord High Executioner on February 13, his 94th birthday, in Halifax, Yorkshire, England. Before retiring in 1979 he reigned for two decades, carrying on the genuine traditions of the old D'Oyly Carte Opera Company, which gave up its ghost in 1982. He's the one who will be missed."

Obituary Column, AMERICAN RECORD GUIDE, May/June 2010

JOHN REED Close House, England, February 13, 1916 — Halifax, England, February 13, 2010 The much-beloved principal comedian of the D'Oyly Carte Opera Company for twenty years, Reed was an agile exponent of all the great Gilbert and Sullivan patter roles, including Ko-Ko in The Mikado, Reginald Bunthorne in Patience, Jack Point in The Yeomen of the Guard and The Lord Chancellor in Iolanthe. Reed joined D'Oyly Carte in 1951 and succeeded Peter Pratt as principal comedian in 1959, eventually recording all of his great roles with the company for Decca between 1960 and 1979, the year he decided to leave the company. Reed later appeared in patter roles with the Washington Opera and with the New York Gilbert & Sullivan Players.

Opera News USA, May 2010

From The Times , March 6, 2010

John Reed: Principal baritone with the D'Oyly Carte. Between 1959, when he made his debut with the D'Oyly Carte Opera Company at the Savoy Theatre as principal comic baritone, and 1979, when he and the company went their separate ways, John Reed was the most famous Savoyard of his generation, both throughout Britain and as far afield as Australasia and North America.

He was, quite simply, a phenomenon. For 48 gruelling weeks of each of those 20 years he effortlessly negotiated the tongue-twisting patter songs introduced to the world by George Grossmith Jr and, later, Frank Wyatt and Walter Passmore, crowning a tradition continued in unbroken succession by C. H. Workman, Henry Lytton, Martyn Green, Grahame Clifford and Reed's immediate predecessor, Peter Pratt.

Reed was typically modest about his voice. It was a light, dry instrument, of the sort often assumed by prim classics masters but ideally fit for purpose and capable, when required, of surprising force and tenderness. His Jack Point, the lovelorn jester in The Yeomen of the Guard, and the role which he dubbed "the one apart, the Hamlet of Gilbert and Sullivan", could easily bring a tear to the eye, as did his spoken rendition of "Iolanthe, thou livest?", the Lord Chancellor's response on learning Iolanthe to be his daughter (wife) and which suddenly reveals a hitherto undisclosed facet of the character's personality.

But he was best known for his comic skills, his impish personality and the dexterity with which he dispatched the famous patter songs. No two of the songs were alike, and Reed recalled the difficulty of learning the Major-General's song with its somewhat disconnected train of thought when compared with the Nightmare Song, the first Gilbert and Sullivan song he worked on.

An all-round, self-taught performer, Reed was as fleet of foot as he was nimble of voice. "I like anything where the dancing comes in. I must say that, because however I worry about words and music — as anybody can — I never ever worry about the dancing. I could fall flat on my bottom and it wouldn't bother me at all. But I can miss a word and I'm upset."

His stage business was an integral part of his interpretations, and the encores in which he participated were eagerly anticipated by his fans, many of whom knew every word of the libretto and were quick to note the slightest verbal slip. As the evening proceeded, his antics would become ever more outrageous, often to the displeasure of the formidable Bridget D'Oyly Carte, and wilfully inventive. In the famous "Bell Trio" from HMS Pinafore, Reed's Sir Joseph Porter would jump overboard only to re-enter clutching a rubber life- ring, while in The Mikado his Ko-Ko would be found furiously — and anachronistically — pedalling across the stage in a toy car.

Ko-Ko was, in fact, his favourite part "because it's such fun to do and you know that you're getting all the reaction that you want from them, and you make people laugh, and the children and everybody enjoy him. And I suppose that's what our job is here anyway — to entertain people."

He contrasted the affable, ageless Ko-Ko with the pompous, ageing Sir Joseph Porter, a part which he "had to work harder on, because they were so non-me, you see. He's a snob and he's always correct and I'm quite the reverse."

In the 1970s Reed added three roles to his repertory: John Wellington Wells in The Sorcerer, unstaged by the company since a fire destroyed the sets, and Scaphio and Grand Duke Rudolph in the 1975 centenary revivals of Utopia Limited and The Grand Duke, works unperformed by the company since the original productions in the 1890s.

During the Reed years the company travelled unceasingly throughout Britain and Ireland, usually performing six evenings a week and often, additionally, matinees. There were also 11 overseas tours, usually to the US and Canada, at first by sea and latterly by air, culminating with a 14-week visit to Australasia in 1979. It was during the latter that he resigned, without ceremony, from the company, prompted by a sense that the D'Oyly Carte was no longer the "family" that it once had been. And so in September of that year he quietly bowed out.

But his career was far from over. Work with the D'Oyly Carte, as stand-in, continued, with Reed himself now dictating the terms. On several occasions he returned as a guest artist, as Sir Joseph, General Stanley, the Lord Chancellor, and Ko-Ko, as well as appearing as a soloist in the Company's "Last Night" concert.

Away from the D'Oyly Carte, Reed continued to perform in, and direct, Gilbert & Sullivan productions. The show A Song to Sing O, devoted to the life and work of George Grossmith, whose mantle he had so memorably inherited, was created for and premiered by him at the Savoy Theatre in 1981. In 1983 he appeared with Washington Opera as the Learned Judge and, singing in French, as Monsieur Balandard in a double bill of Trial by Jury and Offenbach's Monsieur Choufleuri. In the 1980s he made guest appearances with the New York Gilbert & Sullivan Players and directed several G&S productions for the University of Colorado, which awarded him an honorary doctorate.

After retiring from the stage, Reed moved to Halifax, with his partner and business manager, Nicholas Kerri. But G&S still cast its enduring spell and he enjoyed directing amateur G&S societies, including the West Yorkshire Savoyards and, until his eyesight began to fail, productions at the Buxton-based Gilbert and Sullivan Festival.

The Independent, Monday, 1 March 2010

John Reed: Comic lead of the D'Oyly Carte

Many Gilbert & Sullivan fans regarded John Reed, comic lead of the D'Oyly Carte Opera Company for 20 years from 1959 to 1979, as absolutely the best there had ever been in the baritone patter-song roles. Yet when he went to Glasgow to audition for the company in 1951 it was as "an experiment". ......

Reed said that of all his Gilbert and Sullivan roles the one he probably liked, and developed, best was Ko-Ko: "Ko-Ko is almost me. There's a lot of me in the character. It lets me bring out my own sense of humour." But the one he identified with most closely was Jack Point in The Yeomen of the Guard, who, he was convinced, died of a broken heart (the stage direction says only that Jack "falls senseless").

"That really is me," he said. "Jack Point is me in another age – just a strolling player. I really believe I could die of a broken heart, and after the final scene I don't want Jack to stand up for the curtain calls". Reed wanted Jack, instead, to be borne Hamlet-like from the stage (a conceit producers were reluctant to indulge), acknowledging: "Every comedian wants to know they have the ability to make people cry as well as laugh."

The bits of business and topical interpolations he invented in his encores to provoke additional laughter were notorious.

Reed invested all his parts with inventive wit, subtle expression and great comic timing. He was not, he admitted, the greatest of singers, the best of dancers or the most gifted of actors, but he reckoned to make the most of what he had got to maximise the audience's enjoyment. "It's the accumulation that counts," he said, "the sum of all the parts."

He regretted not being given the chance to play the Mikado, traditionally reserved for bigger men. "I could do it. I could be imperious and terrifying," he insisted. "After all, the Japanese aren't a big race, are they?"

For what he regarded as his toughest role, J.W. Wells in The Sorcerer, he was required to act in cockney, a far remove from his native northern accent. He managed it to great comic effect, but did not attempt to carry cockney into the breathtakingly fast patter songs for which accuracy of enunciation was essential.

His least favourite role was probably the hunch-backed and monstrous King Gama in Princess Ida, for whom he felt rather sorry. His principal objection to the part, though, was the heavy make-up that hid every feature of his face except his eyes, and made it impossible for him to wear his glasses so that he could do his newspaper crossword while waiting to go on.

The D'Oyly Carte's 1975 centenary season brought him the opportunity to tackle two more roles, Scaphio in Utopia, Limited and Grand Duke Rudolph in The Grand Duke, works which were revived that year for the first time since their original productions in the 1890s.

During his time with the company Reed undertook 11 overseas tours, 10 as principal comedian. He always claimed that the company was one big family. For a time it was "the Bag family" with many of the members and staff being given "bag" nicknames, so that Reed was "Gasbag", his leading lady "Old Bag", the wardrobe mistress "Laundry Bag", the jobbing understudy "Carrier Bag" and so on. But when abroad, Reed conceded, he had to play the star and be available for interviews and photography, making the tours even more exhausting.

Off-stage, Reed insisted, he was a shy and private person, hiding behind the crossword in a corner when eating alone in restaurants, and often driving long distances from provincial theatres to spend time in his own flat.

Reed left D'Oyly Carte in 1979. He worked in specially created shows and Gilbert and Sullivan performances in Britain and America, but returned as guest artist with D'Oyly Carte several times after his retirement. He took part in the company's "last night" performance when it succumbed to economic pressures and closed in 1982.

After retirement Reed moved to Halifax, where he directed local amateur performances by the West Yorkshire Savoyards and others, and productions at the International Gilbert and Sullivan Festival in Buxton, Derbyshire, as recently as 2004. **Robin Young**

"Melodies For You" on BBC Radio 2 on Sunday February 28th, Alan Titchmarsh popular British TV presenter gave a short tribute to John Reed, and played recordings of John performing, "My name is John Wellington Wells" and "I am the very model".

"On the 13th of February, just two weeks ago, the musical world lost a man who was for my money the finest exponent of the Gilbert & Sullivan patter roles. His name was John Reed and that very day, the 13th of February, was his 94th birthday. Born near Bishop Auckland, County Durham in 1916, John Reed joined D'Oyly Carte in 1951 and took over the patter roles in 1959 from Peter Pratt. He played them all for twenty years, retiring in 1979, after which he lived near Halifax, directing local societies in G&S. His diction, as you heard there, was faultless, and he was the nimblest of dancers, as well as having a great gift for comedy. Mrs T and I saw him many, many times during the early 1970s, and I remember going to see him as a lad up at Leeds Grand [Theatre], I think it must have been, when I was 13 or 14.

"I shall continue to play him on Sunday evenings, hoping the pleasure he's given me over the years is passed on to a new generation of G&S fans. He was, simply, the best" said Mr. Titchmarsh.

The New York Times

John Reed, a silver-tongued Gilbert and Sullivan singer renowned for urbanity, verbal inanity, touching humanity, antic insanity and (a noteworthy trait in a world-famous player quite used to performing for crowned heads of state) a singular lack of theatrical vanity, died in Halifax, England, on Feb. 13, his 94th birthday.

His death was reported by The Press Association, the British news service.......The D'Oyly Carte folded in 1982; though it later had a sputtering revival, it now appears dormant. Mr.Reed, whose work is preserved on its recordings from the 1960s and '70s, was widely seen as the last significant link to the company in its Victorian-tinged glory days.

A butcher's son from the north of England, Mr. Reed was a largely self-taught stage performer who fell into Gilbert and Sullivan by chance. He did not have a trained operatic voice and, in many interviews over the years, was the first to admit it. His light baritone was, fittingly, reedy and could sometimes fail him in the upper registers.

But for a generation of fans, Mr. Reed was the memorable embodiment of Gilbert and Sullivan's "little man" roles, among them John Wellington Wells, the title character of "The Sorcerer"; Major-General Stanley, the very model of etcetera from "The Pirates of Penzance"; Ko-Ko, the nebbish turned lord high executioner in "The Mikado," a part he also played in the 1967 film version.

Mr. Reed was only the fifth man to inhabit those roles regularly for the D'Oyly Carte, following the company's celebrated comics George Grossmith, Henry Lytton, Martyn Green and Peter Pratt. Critics worldwide praised him for his bell-clear diction; dry, sophisticated humor; and nuanced portrayals of characters originally written as outsize satires.

Among the attributes that equipped Mr. Reed spectacularly well for the job were an elfin physique, fleetness of foot (he had been a prize-winning ballroom dancer as a young man) and, perhaps most important, the elocution lessons he had taken in his youth, which let him sail through the rapid-fire patter songs that are the hallmarks of Gilbert and Sullivan's comic baritone roles.

Mr. Reed, who performed for the royal family many times, was appointed to the Order of the British Empire in 1977. After retiring from the D'Oyly Carte in 1979, he performed and directed Gilbert and Sullivan with opera companies in the United States and elsewhere. With the Washington Opera he sang the role of Menelaus in Offenbach's comic operetta "La Belle Hélène" in 1983.

Mr. Reed's only immediate survivor is his companion of more than half a century, Nicholas Kerri, The Press Association reported.

Over his two decades as the D'Oyly Carte's star, Mr. Reed acquired such a command of Gilbert's clatter of consonants that even the most fiendish patter song became, if not quite routine, at least comfortably familiar.

"It's funny how the brain works," he told The Associated Press in 1988.

"I can be standing there singing the Nightmare Song from 'Iolanthe'

looking out at a woman in the audience wearing a hat and thinking, 'My God, that hat is so big the man behind her can't see.' And the words keep coming with no problem."

Master of the 'patter' roles and principal comedian with D'Oyly Carte for 20 years

---

The Guardian

John Reed, who has died on his 94th birthday, was for 20 years the principal comedian of the D'Oyly Carte Opera Company. His comic timing, nimble footwork and clarity of diction made him the acknowledged master of the "patter" roles, at once the most challenging and defining of all Gilbert and Sullivan's creations.

Reed was the last great D'Oyly Carte patter man in a tradition that stretched back through Martyn Green and Henry Lytton to George Grossmith. Spare of frame and fleet-footed, he was an endearingly energetic Ko-Ko in the Mikado, but also had the acting ability to bring out the pathos of the character of the Lord Chancellor in Iolanthe, the narcissism of Reginald Bunthorne in Patience and the misanthropy of King Gama in Princess Ida. He is the only principal artist in the history of the D'Oyly Carte company to have recorded every one of the 13 Savoy operas and his light, clear voice lives on in the CD reissues of the Decca LPs made during the 1960s and 1970s.

The company of which he was now the leading member was in some respects a Victorian survival, run on the principles of a strict boarding school. There were 48 weeks of performance each year, many of them at provincial touring venues that were reached by specially chartered trains with separate, reserved carriages for principals, female chorus, male chorus, orchestra, management and stage staff. Dressing rooms for the different sexes were always sited, if possible, on opposite sides of the stage. Reed recalled that for sound-recording sessions throughout the 1960s, the male chorus were expected to wear suits and most of the ladies would wear hats. He also remarked that "no lady would ever turn up to a rehearsal in trousers".

Although some aspects of the tightly controlled regime, where principals were not allowed to vary or change the smallest gesture or stage move, niggled him, Reed loved the family atmosphere that the touring life engendered and developed many close friendships with members of the company that continued throughout his life. He participated in lengthy tours of North America and Australasia. His fans included the Queen, who would sometimes slip into performances unannounced, and Harold Wilson, whose advocacy, he suspected, played a part in the award of an OBE in 1977.

Daily Telegraph John Reed, who died on February 13, his 94th birthday, was the principal comic baritone with the D'Oyly Carte Opera Company for two decades.

He made his debut with the company in 1951 as a member of the chorus and understudy to Peter Pratt for the principal comedy parts, filling in for roles such as Major-General Stanley in The Pirates of Penzance, Reginald Bunthorne in Patience, the Lord Chancellor in Iolanthe, and Ko-Ko in The Mikado.

In 1959 Pratt left the company, and Reed replaced him, continuing to perform the role of the "patter man", or principal comedian, until 1979 and entertaining audiences in London, Australia, the United States and Canada with his renditions of Gilbert and Sullivan's fast-paced lyrics.

One of his performances in HMS Pinafore was described in The Times as "prim, dry, roundly articulated (and sung in tune, as some of his illustrious predecessors never attempted to do)".

In later life he lived in Halifax, West Yorkshire, where he directed the local Gilbert and Sullivan society, the West Yorkshire Savoyards. He was also closely involved in the annual International Gilbert and Sullivan Festival at Buxton, Derbyshire.

John Reed is survived by his partner of 52 years, Nicholas Kerri.

From Australia....

I received the news of John's death in Canberra, the capital of Australia and the place that the D'Oyly Carte opened its one tour of Oz in 1979. So many memories came flooding back, of that tour and so much else.

John had only taken on the patter roles a couple of years before I first began seeing the company. There were still those who would say that he wasn't a patch on his predecessors (and for them it would be true, a first love is hard to replace) but I thought he was absolutely wonderful. The cheeky personae, the lithe energetic performances, his ability to get through the patter songs with every word clear and the roguishness of his sense of humour were all immediately attractive.

As the years progressed and I became a regular at the company's performances and got to know many of the singers, my admiration for all of them was unbounded, but John was king! I remember him looking at me one day and saying "you've grown up! You were just a little girl when we first saw you!".

Over the years I saw him in a role in every opera - he did the Judge in Trial for the Centenary season and also appeared in Utopia and the concert version of Grand Duke. He didn't necessarily have the best voice and did have a habit of getting out of time with the music, but he still shone.

When the company came to Australia I had made arrangements to do go to Canberra for the opening night but on the day they arrived and were given the weekend to recover from the long flight, John was flown to Melbourne to do a TV talk show. I didn't know about that, but I was in the city that night leaving a theatre when I saw John being taken down to meet some of the actors in that show. As he walked past me I said "Welcome to Australia, Mr Reed". He swung round in surprise and said "I have just arrived and am recognised already - that's lovely". He was accompanied by Derek Glynn, the manager who had brought out the company, who was just delighted at this joy from a potential audience member.

At the time I was doing a weekly radio programme covering theatre in Melbourne and was of course given tickets to all the performances and the publicist knew I had a particular interest in G&S. In Canberra I was given access to all the company to do interviews. John told me a story about a TV appearance he had made in the US, when a certain women had panned the company. Thinking he was waiting for the camera to start rolling he was asked about this woman's review and he started making remarks about her like: she's older than God, so what do you expect. But of course all this was going to air and he was mortified!

It was during the time the Co were in Melbourne that rumours began circulating that John had decided to retire at the end of the Oz tour. I knew that there would be many UK fans who would be disappointed that they had no chance to say goodbye, so I asked the publicist if I could do one long interview as a retrospect of his career. I was invited to his hotel room on the last day the company were in Melbourne. There was a matinee of The Mikado but Conroy Ward was on. John was doing his ironing as I arrived and, finishing it, began to do some sewing repairs as I turned on the mike and began the interview. As John folded his ironing he showed me a hankie which had Jack Point embroidered in the corner and said it had been a present from a fan and then he threw it on my lap and said "You have it". It is still among my treasures. I have 2 other souvenirs of that tour. I went to Adelaide for the company's time there and John did his last KoKo as a member of the company. I asked a friend in the chorus if she would pinch one of the flowers that bloom in the spring for me. She asked John if it would be OK and he handed her a small bunch of the flowers - which of course I still have.

Later in the year, John was called back for some guest appearances when both Conroy Ward and Alastair Donkin were ill - I don't know what he did for the flowers!

An Adelaide newspaper had taken a lot of photos of the company in HMS Pinafore costumes and I went with one of the principals to look at them and ordered a few including one of John as Sir Joseph. The pics were posted to the aforementioned principal who took the one of John as Sir J into his dressing room, on my request, for a dated autograph.

When I received it he had written "Best wishes always, signed while making up for my last performance as a member of the D'Oyly Carte Opera Company" You can imagine how much I value that.

John used to joke that when he first took over the parts he found Robin Oakapple a straight role and the Chancellor a character one. By the 1970s it was the other way round! His talent for entertaining, his sense of humour and his most delightful personality will be sorely missed. On my 500 k drive to Canberra I played The Gondoliers constantly on the car CD, each time we got to the cachucha I would see John's wonderful creative dancing in the encores (until Besch cut them out).

The Gondoliers indeed gives me the ideal sign out - John, we leave you with feelings of pleasure. **Diana Burleigh**

From Hancock County, Maine, USA

We first met John Reed in Boston in the 70's when he appeared with the D'OC on tour there. His Bell Trio and subsequent encores filled the audience with gut-busting laughter, making it almost impossible for the show to continue. He was all his recordings promised he would be, and even more. As we walked out of the theatre, we had no idea of the pleasure he would bring us years later in Buxton.

We took our UTOPIA, LTD to Buxton in the first year of the Festival, and to our horror, we learned on the first night that the performances would be adjudicated. Silly Yanks, we thought the word

"Festival" signified a fun time, a "ball for all and nothing small".

Little did we know that we would be subject to David Turner's

microscope and incisive wit on the last night of the performances.

During the course of the Festival, at the Festival Club following the performances, amid "pie and peas" and Bass Ale, we were able to thank John Reed in person for the unforgettable Boston performance and to share our anxiety about coming across the pond with a show that would be adjudicated in the very country where it was first performed. John just laughed it off and encouraged us to have a lot of fun among a very special group of thespians.

During the two weeks we saw him about the town, at rehearsals, at the shows, and of course, the Festival Club. He became a good friend of our company, and was backstage with us before our UTOPIA, LTD.

performance. We had talked about the 'energy circle" we employed as a company just before the curtain rose, in which the entire company would gather on stage, form a circle and hold hands with the person on either side. Sometimes someone would offer a comment, but most of the time we just let the energy of the company pass from one member to the next, all around the circle, as we focused on the task at hand. When we got into position before the curtain went up on UTOPIA, John asked if he could join us in the circle. We were gobsmacked; here was the patter king of the D'OC asking if he could join the energy circle of

an unknown company from the wilds of Maine in the northeast corner
of the United States as it made its final preparations to go on stage.
We had never felt so honored by a request as we did at that moment.
His inclusion in our energy circle made us forget about our jitters as we
all realized what a special moment we were all experiencing that night.
The result was we put out our best effort and delivered a show that
appealed to the audience as well as to David Turner.

John, you, indeed, had a song to sing-o, and you sang it faithfully and
well. We were privileged to have known you and we now all attend to
you, shedding more than a tear or two. Thank you, John.
Steve Johnson

Before the overture of every D'Oyly Carte performance the sometimes
strange sounds of vocal exercises filled the backstage corridors. But
from the dressing room of John Reed just one short vowel might be
heard, somewhere in the middle of the voice, followed by "That'll do."

John didn't think of himself as a singer. "I'm a dancer really. My
singing voice is an extension of my speaking. As so often, John was
being modest and self-effacing. Two examples of his eloquently
expressive singing come to mind: his moving account of "Tit Willow"
and his poignant last scene in Yeomen.

John was very kind when I joined the D'Oyly Carte, doing everything
he could to help me settle in. After a period of intense rehearsals he
waited until my debut as Nanki-Poo was successfully over before he
moved to the next level of my "acclimatization." During the second act
of another performance of the Mikado shortly after, Ko-Ko said:
"I can't kill you – I can't kill anything – I can't kill anybody" and came
to sob on my shoulder. Before I could reply "Come my poor fellow"
I felt a gently but unmistakable nipping of my rear end by John's
upstage hand. Surprise helped me keep my face straight. I took it that
John wanted me to feel accepted as part of "the family," who frequently
teased each other surreptitiously onstage.

John himself was teased at every performance of The Gondoliers. In the Duke's first scene, Jon Ellison would enter as a dapper waiter with a tureen of spaghetti that he placed on the table in front of John. Then with a flourish "Elli" would remove the lid to reveal the spaghetti – and an object that his ingenious imagination had introduced. At one performance it was a set of false teeth made of pink candy. John took it in his stride.

At the stage door after performances fans would ask me " Has John left yet?" When I went to check and John was aware that someone was waiting especially to see him, he would ask me to bring them to his dressing room for a chat.

Now John has left for the last time. But he remains in the loving memory of the thousands whose lives he touched with his artistry, his ready smile and his sense of fun.

Geoffrey Shovelton.

Foot note

After John had left the D'Oyly Carte, they were playing in Nottingham and his successor James Conroy Ward was taken ill and his understudy Alastair Donkin was unable to be present. They had a very major problem on their hands. The theatre was full and an announcement had to be made. It was made along the following lines: 'Ladies and Gentlemen, we are very sorry to announce that Mr Conroy Ward is unable to appear as the Major General this evening, and we are also very sorry that Mr Donkin is unavailable. At very short notice we hope you will accept their replacement, Mr John Reed.' The theatre erupted with pleasure and excitement. That was the capacity of Dear John Reed.

Nicholas Kerri
Gilvan
260 Claremount Road
Halifax
West Yorkshire
HX3 6AW

I'll be With You
to The End of the World

I'll be near you, I will love you
If you need me, only call me
And I'll be there at your side
And I'll bring peace, peace, peace
Yes I'll bring you peace, peace, peace.

I will love you to the end of your days.
I'll be near you, I'll watch o'er you.
And when sorrows over whelm you
only call me – I'll be there.
And I'll bring peace, peace, peace
I'll bring you peace, peace, peace

And when death comes at the end of the world
I'll be near you, you'll be near me.
And you'll see me and you'll touch me
And you'll be here at my side
And there'll be peace, peace, peace
Yes there'll be peace, peace, peace.

Dedicated to *John* by *Nicholas*

*This moving poem, selected by Nicki was read by David Steadman
at John's funeral service*